Anonymous

Lizzie's Cook Book

Anonymous

Lizzie's Cook Book

ISBN/EAN: 9783744788717

Printed in Europe, USA, Canada, Australia, Japan

Cover: Foto ©Lupo / pixelio.de

More available books at **www.hansebooks.com**

LIZZIE'S

COOK BOOK

―――EDITED BY―――

"THE BACHELETTE."

SAN JOSE, SANTA CLARA CO., CALIFORNIA
SMITH & WILCOX PRINTERS.
1891.

To
The Friend
In Whose Pleasant Home
These Recipes
Were "Tried" and Found To Be "True"
This Book
Is Affectionately Dedicated.

PREFACE.

EVERYBODY knows Lizzie! She is one of the best cooks in town. I am sure of this, for "The proof of the pudding is in the eating," and I have eaten. Her puddings are delicious, delicate, wholesome. In fact, I am a living monument to her skill.

It seems a pity to waste such talents on a few individuals and it is my pleasant mission to acquaint a suffering, dyspeptic world with the virtues of Lizzie's well cooked dishes, spiced now and then with some of her pithy sayings.

Many cook books are too elaborate and confusing. They seem to be written for people, who live with great ceremony; who have retinues of servants at dinner, bringing in turtle soup and turkey, silver chafing-dishes and gold spoons. But, the majority of Americans do not live in this way at all; they are glad to have beefsteak and bread; wedgewood ware and one good servant. It is for this great majority, that "Lizzie's Cook Book" is written.

No recipes will be found here for the dishes set before the Duke of Nocastle, when Mrs. Smith of Smithville entertained him and so incurred the undying enmity of her neighbors. But there are recipes, clear and exact, we hope, for getting good breakfasts, luncheons, dinners and suppers for people who live simply and rationally.

The purpose is, to make this book, in one respect at least, like Wordsworth's "perfect woman,"

> "Not too wise nor good,
> For human nature's daily food."

With the recipes for cooking, are a few plain directions for marketing, for Lizzie markets as well as she cooks. When she starts off with the market basket on her arm, the good things of life seem to come out to meet her.

Her searching, merry blue eye looks around the market or fruit store and spies all the tid-bits hidden away for the favorite customer or for the millionaire's table. Then she smiles her winsome smile at the market man and praises his baby; he can no more help bringing out those "goodies," than a fly can help going into a spider's net.

> "Everything good and nothing harmful."

That "Lizzie's Cook Book" may be helpful "in the hour of need" is the sincere hope of

"THE BACHELETTE."

[The authors desire to present their cordial acknowledgments to the skillful young stenographer and typewriter, Miss Nora Hall of Del Norte, whose kind assistance has turned the labor of composition into a pleasure.]

Go, little Book, and wend thy way,
    Through city, mart and lane,
Maidens perchance, and women grey,
    May read thee, not in vain.

Of dishes, spiced by mother wit,
    To tell the world, thou'rt able,
And on thy leaves are fairly writ,
    Good tidings for the table.

HOW TO SELECT GOOD FLOUR.

"It don't pay to buy poor flour to make good bread, because you can't make it."

Good flour may be known by its soft, friendly feeling. Rub it through your fingers and it has no grit. Pinch it into a figure and it keeps its shape. Throw a little on the wall, and, if good, it will stick like the paper balls, which naughty children throw at the school-room ceiling. Sometimes it has a yellowish color, then again it isn't so yellow and is just as good.

It is best for young housekeepers to buy flour in small quantities, until they have learned to select it well, or, have found a reliable brand. Some millers never send out anything but good flour, and their trade-mark is never questioned, which shows that "Honesty is the best policy," for the miller as well as for other people, though some millers never find that out.

BREAD.

It's half in the making and half in the baking.

The making of bread is no small matter, for to make it good, takes time, strength and thought. Give a man good bread and butter and he will not ask for pies and cakes.

The first thing is to buy good flour. Directions already given.

WHITE BREAD.

Flour, ... 3 qts.
Potatoes, 2 (boiled and mashed fine while hot.)
Warm milk, ...2 qts.
Or warm water, .2 qts.
Sugar, ... 1 tablespoonful.
Fine salt, ... 1 dessertspoonful.
Compressed yeast, ... ½ cake.

Dissolve the yeast in a little luke warm water, then stir, or rather, beat all together in the bread pan. Set the pan where the sponge will keep moderately warm, but do not let it get hot. In three hours it should be light enough to knead. Add flour and knead into a dough stiff enough not to stick to the pan. Let it rise again, keeping it warm. Then mold into five loaves, put into pans well greased with good butter let it rise for third and last time, and then bake in a moderately hot oven for about one hour.

Some housekeepers prefer to set the sponge at night, knead the dough early in the morning and bake during the forenoon. There is a little risk of its souring or rising too much, in this way.

Others set the sponge in the morning—seven o'clock is a good hour—knead into dough about ten o'clock; mold into loaves and put in the oven about one o'clock. Both ways are good and you take your choice.

Graham Bread.

Fine white flour,	1 qt.
Salt,	1 teaspoonful.
Compressed yeast,	½ cake.
Warm water,	1 pint.

Dissolve yeast in a little warm water, stir all well together and set to rise in a warm place. When well risen, take a half cup of molasses, one tablespoonful of butter, and Graham flour enough to make a good stiff batter. Stir well with a spoon, then set to rise again. When light, put without kneading into pans, let them stand until the dough rises to the top of the pans, then bake in a hot oven about three-quarters of an hour.

Boston Brown Bread.

Good corn meal,	1 cup.
Rye or Graham,	1 cup.
Molasses,	½ cup
Salt,	1 teaspoonful.
Sour milk,	1 cup.
Butter,	1 tablespoonful.
Soda,	1 teaspoonful.

Beat all well together. Grease a quart can or mold, pour the batter into it, cover and steam three hours. Very good.

Graham Gems (No. 1.)

Graham flour,	1 pt.
Water,	1 pt.

Put the graham flour in a bowl, stirring in the water gradually. Have the gem pans and oven *very hot*, for on this depends the success of the gems. Bake twenty minutes.

Graham Gems (No. 2.)

White flour,	½ cup.
Graham flour,	1 cup.
Molasses,	1 tablespoonful.
Salt,	½ teaspoonful.
Butter,	1 tablespoonful.
Eggs,	1.
Baking powder,	2 teaspoonfuls.

Beat well. Heat the gem-pans hot and bake in quick oven.

Gallagher Mary's Muffins.

Take a bowl and break one egg into it.

Sugar,	1 tablespoonful.
Salt,	½ teaspoonful.
Butter,	1 tablespoonful.

Beat well together, then add one pint of sweet milk, two cups of sifted flour with one heaping teaspoonful of baking powder. Beat all well together and pour into warm muffin rings. Bake in slow oven about twenty minutes.

Breakfast Rolls.

Take from the bread dough, enough to make one loaf. Add to this·

>One tablespoonful of sugar.
>One tablespoonful of melted butter or lard.

Set away to rise, where it is cool. When well risen, roll on a board, cut in pieces large enough to make a good sized biscuit. Roll the pieces out flat, put a little melted butter on each piece and fold over once. Lay them in a greased pan and set away to rise again. Bake about twenty minutes in a moderate oven. When done, take from the pan and lay in a clean napkin until served.

Parker House Rolls.

>Scalded milk, ... 1 pint.
>Compressed yeast, . . . ½ cake.
>Melted butter, ... ½ cup.
>Sugar, ... 1 tablespoonful.
>Salt, ... ½ teaspoonful.
>Eggs, ... 1.
>Flour, ... 2½ cups.

Begin at two o'clock in the afternoon if you wish to have them for breakfast next morning. Sift flour into pan, make a little hole in the flour, put in milk, salt, and yeast dissolved in a little warm water. Stir gently from the middle, leaving some of the flour around the edges. Set to rise in a moderately warm place. About eight o'clock in the evening add butter, sugar and egg. Stir well, add flour and mold into a stiff dough. Set in a cool place and cover with a clean napkin. In the morning about one hour before breakfast, make into rolls, folding each one over a little melted butter. Let them rise, and bake twenty minutes in a hot oven, just in time for breakfast.

Baking Powder Biscuits.

Flour,	1 pint.
Warm milk,	1 pint.
Salt,	½ teaspoonful.
Baking powder,	2 teaspoonfuls.
Butter,	1 tablespoonful.

Put the flour and salt in the bowl, rub in the butter with the hand and add the milk. Sift the baking powder into a half-cup of flour and add to the mixture, working gently with the hand until the dough is flexible, but not stiff. Roll out an inch thick, cut with a biscuit cutter and bake in a moderately hot oven.

White Gems.

Flour (sifted,)	2½ cups.
Milk (sweet,)	1 pint.
Eggs,	1.
Salt,	½ teaspoonful.
Butter or lard,	1 tablespoonful.
Sugar,	1 tablespoonful.
Baking powder,	2 teaspoonfuls.

Beat the eggs, salt, butter and sugar together, add the milk, sift the baking powder into the flour and stir in gently. Pour into hot gem pans and bake in a quick oven.

Hygienic Batter Cakes.

Stale bread,	½ loaf.
Sour milk,	1½ pints.
Salt,	½ teaspoonful.

GRIDDLE CAKES.

Baking powder,............ 1 teaspoonful.
Eggs,............................. 1.
Sifted flour,.................... 1 cup.

Soak the bread over night in a pint of sour milk. In the morning, beat the eggs and salt into the bread, dissolve the soda in the rest of the sour milk, add a cup of sifted flour, beat all well together and bake on a hot, well greased griddle.

RICE GRIDDLE CAKES.

Cold Boiled Rice,............ 1 cup.
Salt,......................... 1/2 teaspoonful.
Sweet milk,................... 1 pint.
Baking powder,........ 1 full teaspoonful.
Flour (sifted),................ 2 cups.
Eggs,......................... 3.

Beat the eggs, rice and salt together. Add the milk and sift baking powder into the flour. Beat all well together and bake on hot, well greased griddle. Serve immediately.

WELCH GRIDDLE CAKES.

Eggs............................. 6.
Milk,......................... 1 pint.
Flour,........................ 1 pint.
Salt,......................... 1/2 teaspoonful.

Beat the yolks and white separately, then add milk and salt to the yolks and gradually stir in flour, beating constantly. Lastly, add the whites, beating all together. Have the griddle very hot and well buttered. Butter the cakes when taken from the griddle and serve immediately.

SALLY LUNN.

Flour,	1 quart.
Milk,	½ pint.
Eggs,	2.
Butter,	Size of an egg.
Sugar,	3 tablespoonfuls.
Baking powder,	2 teaspoonfuls.

Mix thoroughly and bake twenty minutes.

POP-OVERS.

Flour,	3 cups.
Milk,	3 cups.
Eggs,	3.
Salt,	1 pinch.

Beat eggs until very light; add one cup milk. Add the flour, stirring briskly to make a thick paste, then gradually add remainder of milk. Heat and butter gem tins and drop in the batter. Bake in a quick oven.

WAFFLES.

Sour milk,	1 pint.
Eggs,	2.
Salt,	½ teaspoonful.
Soda,	1 teaspoonful.
Flour,	2 cups.
Melted butter,	1 tablespoonful.

Beat the eggs in the bowl and add milk and salt. Stir in flour gradually, beating all the time. Dissolve the soda in two tablespoonfuls of sour milk and stir in gradually. Have the waffle irons very hot and well greased. Pour in batter and bake quickly. Serve immediately.

CORN BREAD.

Sweet milk,	1 pint.
Sour milk,	1 pint.
White flour,	1 pint.
Corn meal,	2 pints.
Syrup,	1 teaspoonful.
Salt,	½ teaspoonful.
Soda,	1 teaspoonful.

Dissolve soda in sour milk, mix all together and steam three hours.

CORN BREAD, NO. 2.

Eggs,	2.
Sugar,	1 cup.
Butter,	½ cup.
Sweet milk,	1 cup.
Sour milk,	½ cup.
White flour,	½ cup.
Corn meal,	1½ cups.
Baking powder,	2 teaspoonfuls.

Beat all well together and bake in quick oven.

MUSH.

CORN MEAL MUSH.

Take one quart of boiling water and salt to taste. Stir in four tablespoonfuls of meal very slowly to prevent lumps being formed. Add one teaspoonful of salt and cook slowly from one to two hours, adding hot water if needed.

FRIED MUSH.

Pour the mush when cooked into a shallow dish to cool. The next morning, cut into slices and fry on griddle greased with butter to a light brown.

GRAHAM MUSH.

Have ready one quart of boiling water with one-half a teaspoonful of salt. Stir in gradually a pint of Graham flour. Stir all the time to avoid lumps. When well mixed, set where it will not burn and cook slowly a half an hour.

SAGO MUSH.

To one cup of sago, add one pint of boiling milk and a half teaspoonful of salt. Cook in rice boiler adding warm milk as it is required, to keep it from getting too thick. Serve with cream and sugar.

Germea Mush.

Take about one-half pint of germea and put it into a rice boiler, pouring boiling water over it slowly. Add one-half teaspoonful of salt, stirring well at first. Steam for one-half hour. This is also good when cold. Serve with cream and sugar.

Farina Mush.

Add a pint of boiling water slowly to one-half a cup of farina, stirring well to avoid lumps. Add one-half a teaspoonful of salt and boil one-half an hour. This is good cold with cream and sugar.

Whole Wheat Mush.

Put whole wheat to soak for at least twenty-four hours. Then pour into a rice boiler, add boiling water and Cook slowly for about three hours. Serve hot.

Breakfast Delight.

Take about one-half cup of breakfast delight and half a teaspoonful of salt. Pour over it one pint of boiling water gradually, stirring constantly. Put into rice boiler and stir only two or three times, while cooking. Cook quickly for half an hour.

All mushes are better if not stirred while cooking. Do not soak in cold water, unless the grains are whole.

Rolled Oats.

Stir rolled oats into one quart of cold water until of the consistency of very thin mush. Put in rice boiler and cook for about one-half an hour. Seave hot.

BOILED RICE.

Pick one cup of rice over carefully and wash well. Put it in the rice boiler and pour over it one pint of boiling water or milk. Add one-half a teaspoonful of salt and boil for an hour, not stirring, but taking care that it does not burn. Serve as a breakfast mush.

CRACKED WHEAT MUSH.

To one quart salted water, add three quarters of a cup of cracked or hulled wheat, and steam two hours.

HOMINY.

Take one cup of hominy to one quart of salted water. Soak over night and boil three quarters of an hour in the morning. Serve with cream and sugar. Slice and fry when cold.

MEATS.

BEEF.

HOW TO TELL GOOD BEEF.

The best beef is of a clear red color, juicy in appearance, with a fine grain, smooth to the touch. In cold weather it should present a well mixed or marbled appearance. The fat is of a clear, straw color. The suet should be of a brighter shade than the meat fat, dry but not hard; should crumble easily and show little fibre.

The second quality of beef has flesh and fat of a darker color and is of a coarser grain, has less meat to the quantity of bone and is less juicy.

The hind quarters are the choicest parts of the whole beef; from them is cut the famous "Baron of Beef," which is always served at the Christmas dinner of the queen or king of England.

The "Baron of Beef" divided in the center makes two sirloins, which are cut into roasts and sirloin steaks. The tenderloin steak or *fillet de bœuf* is very delicate, but not so nutritious as the regular sirloin steaks. It is better for young housekeepers to find a good reliable butcher and depend upon him, until they have learned the different cuts and qualities of beef and signs of good meat.

ROAST BEEF.

Rib roast or any cut for roasting, should be put into a pan on a wire frame as this protects the meat so that it will not touch the water. Lay the beef on the wire in the pan, salt, pepper and flour it, put into a hot oven with a little water in the bottom of the pan. It will take about one hour to cook an eight pound roast. Baste well, while roasting.

How To Buy Beefsteak.

Never buy meat that is already cut. See the butcher cut it. Beefsteak should be at least two inches thick, with plenty of fat around the edge, and of a good clear red in color. Ask for sirloin, tenderloin or porter-house steak. These are the best and although dear, at first, cheaper in the end, because there is no waste.

How To Broil a Beefsteak.

Here is a rule adopted by the famous Beefsteak Club in London.

> "Pound well your meat until the fibres break;
> Be sure that next you have, to broil the steak,
> Good coals in plenty; nor a moment leave,
> But turn it over this way and then that.
> Then lean should be quite rare—not so the fat;
> The platter now and then the juice receive.
> Put on your butter—place it on your meat
> Salt, pepper; turn it over, serve and eat."

The first direction in this piece of verse, most good cooks of the present day would tell you to neglect. Good steak should never be pounded. Poor steak may be improved by it, if anything can improve it. The following is a better way to cook steak:

Trim off the fat around the edge of the steak, leaving some for cooking. Then slit the edges here and there with a sharp knife. Heat a clean broiler over a bed of clear red coals. Lay the steak on the broiler, and, when one side is well browned, turn the meat and cook the other side brown. Put some butter on a hot plate, lay the steak on it, salt, pepper and serve immediately. Steak should not be put on the fire until the first course is already served. Those who prefer their steak cooked through, with no rare meat, should buy thinner steak.

BEEF A LA MODE.

Select seven pounds of the round of beef and remove the fat from the outside. With a clean skewer, make two holes down through the beef. Cut very thin pieces of salt pork. On them scatter cinnamon, cloves, fine mace and fill the holes in the beef with the pork thus seasoned. Tie the beef then with a cord around and around to form a loaf. Chop two large onions and brown in the skillet in butter, then put in flat bottomed iron pan and lay the loaf in on top of the onions, over which pour a teacup of boiling water. Then salt and pepper. Cook two hours over a slow fire and cover closely, watching that it may not burn. When well done, take up in a deep dish and serve.

BAKED BEEFSTEAK.

Lay the steak in a deep pan. Make a dressing of stale bread broken into small pieces, one small onion, chopped fine, salt, pepper and a piece of butter the size of a walnut. Soak the bread in hot water, then mix all together with a very very little nutmeg. The nutmeg gives a delicious flavor, but there must not be enough to recognize. Mix the stuffing well and lay on one-half the steak, folding the other half over it. Press down the edges. Bake one-half hour in a very hot oven. Place in a hot dish and serve immediately.

Corned Beef.

How to Select Corned Beef.

To test corn beef put a skewer through it, withdraw it, and if the meat is good the fragments that adhere to the skewer will be red and have an agreeable odor.

Corned Beef.

Take from three to five pounds of corn beef, pour boiling water on it, cover tight and boil three hours. Should it be very salt, the water must be changed at least once.

Spanish Tomato Beefsteak.

Take a very thick steak from the round of a beef, cut gashes in it with a sharp knife, fill the holes with powdered cracker crumbs and little bits of butter, then roll up tightly and tie. Pour a quart of tomatoes in a deep sauce-pan and lay the roll of beef into it. Cover closely and cook slowly for two and one-half hours, until the meat is well done. Then untie the roll, lay it on a hot platter, pouring the tomatoes, which will be a thick gravy, around the meat.

Beef Heart.

Clean out the heart and wash well, salt and fill with a bread dressing, as given in baked beefsteak, then put in pan, salt and pepper, and bake in oven for two hours. Very good if properly made.

A Yorkshire Pudding.

For every pint of milk take three eggs, three tablespoonfuls of flour, one pinch of salt. Stir to a batter and pour into the pan under roast beef, half an hour before it is to be taken from the oven. Serve on a plate with the roast.

Irish Stew.

Take about two pounds of beef and mutton, mix and chop into small pieces one inch square. Put into a skillet and cover with cold water. Set over the fire, add two good sized onions, one nice tomato and one small carrot, cut into small square pieces. Boil one and one-half hours. When meat and vegetables are tender, add salt, pepper and four good sized Irish potatoes. Add a piece of butter the size of a walnut, a good tablespoonful of flour mixed well with a little cold water and stir gently into the stew just before taking it off the fire.

This is very good.

MUTTON.

HOW TO CHOOSE GOOD MUTTON.

The fat should be clear and hard, the lean firm, juicy and of a rich, darkish red color. The leg bones clean and lean or quite white.

Poor mutton is seldom fat, or, if plump, the fat has a yellowish appearance, the flesh is flabby, the kidney small and stringy, and the lean, seen through the skin on the back, is of a dark, bluish shade.

If possible select the hind quarter of mutton or lamb, as that is always the best.

Roast Leg of Mutton or Lamb.

Take a good leg of mutton or lamb, wash nicely, put into a pan, salt, pepper and flour it. Then pour a little hot water in the pan and bake in a hot oven for one and one-half hours, basting well all the time to keep the meat from being dry. Should the oven be too hot, place another pan over the meat.

MUTTON CHOPS.

Buy lean chops, cut out all extra fat and scrape the small end of the bones. Have the broiler hot. Broil brown but do not burn. Then salt, pepper and serve on a hot platter. Do not cook until nearly ready to be served.

ROAST MUTTON OR LAMB.

Always, if possible, get the hind quarter of lamb or mutton as that is the best. The fore quarter, however, is very nice. Take out bones, fill with stale crumbs well seasoned as in baked beefsteak. Sew up and bake in a quick oven. It will be fine.

MINCED MUTTON OR LAMB.

Remove fat and bones from cold mutton or lamb and chop fine. To one cup of meat, add salt, pepper and one-half cup of thickened gravy. Put all into the pan, heat a little and serve very hot.

SCALLOPED MUTTON.

Cut cold mutton into thin pieces. Remove all bone, fat and gristle. Place a layer of bread crumbs on the bottom of a shallow dish, then a layer of mutton, then a layer of boiled maccaroni. Then add gravy left from day before. Moisten one cup of crumbs with one tablespoonful of butter. Scatter this on the top and bake about twenty minutes until brown.

VEAL.
HOW TO CHOOSE GOOD VEAL.

The fat should be white and clear, the lean pink or flesh color. White veal or that from calves less than six weeks old is not suitable for food.

ROAST VEAL.

The principal thing in cooking veal is to have it well done. Take about three pounds of veal from the leg, salt, pepper, put in a pan with some butter. Dredge a little flour on it and bake in a hot oven. It requires about two hours to cook it well.

VEAL CUTLETS.

Try to get the loin cutlets, as they are always the best. Take about six good cutlets, one egg and some cracker crumbs. Put some butter on the bottom of a pan, heat it very hot and cook the cutlets slowly. Take them up when well done and lay on a hot platter, but do not cover them. Keep hot until served.

VEAL STEW.

Take about two pounds of veal from the ribs and cut into small pieces. Put pieces into a pan, cover with cold water and let them simmer slowly for about one hour. Then salt and pepper. Wet one tablespoonful of flour with cold water and stir in slowly. Then, if you wish to have dumplings, take one cup of flour, one-half teaspoonful of salt, one egg, one-half cup of sweet milk, one teaspoonful of baking powder. Mix well and drop into the meat, cover tightly and cook for about fifteen minutes. It will then be ready to serve.

VEAL LOAF.

Take three pounds of lean veal, boil in a little water and chop fine with a quarter of a pound of salt pork, two eggs well beaten and one cup of rolled crackers. Salt and pepper to taste. Mix all well together and press down into a deep pan. Set this into a meat pan full of hot water, put in the oven and bake slowly for one hour. When cold cut into thin slices. Very nice for luncheon.

Veal Fricassee.

Buy the ends of the ribs and some of the breast, about two pounds in all. Cut into small pieces, dredge with flour and brown in butter or salt pork fat. Then put into a pot, cover with boiling water, skim as it begins to boil and cook until well done.

Meat Souffle.

Cold meat of any kind is good for this dish. Remove all bones and fat and chop fine. Place a layer of bread crumbs in the bottom of a dish and then a layer of meat. Pepper and butter. Add a little onion or thyme. Then another layer of crumbs and of meat, seasoned as before. Beat one egg well, add to it one pint of milk and pour over the meat. Add more milk if necessary, to bring milk up to the top of the crumbs. Then bake in a hot oven for about one-half hour, until the top is well done.

Stuffed Veal.

Buy about five pounds of the shoulder of veal. Have the blade bone taken out and prepare a stuffing of stale bread. Break one loaf of bread into small pieces, put in a little butter and salt and pepper to taste. Add a little sage, then fill the veal, sew up and spread butter over it. Bake about two hours in hot oven.

Sweet Breads.

Lay the sweet breads in cold water with a little salt before using. Take out of the water and dry thoroughly by pressing gently between folds of clean, soft linen. Have ready a hot pan with butter. After dipping the sweet breads in flour put into the pan and fry brown, serving hot.

Calf's or Sheep's Brains.

Soak the brains over night in cold water with a little salt. In the morning pour off the salt water and plunge them into boiling water. Then skim them very carefully, so as not to break the fibres. Flour them and have ready a pan good and hot with some butter. Fry brown, but do not burn. Some people like them rolled in cracker crumbs instead of flour. Serve hot.

Scrambled Brains.

Clean the brains as above, put into a pan, pour a little water over them, add a good piece of butter, salt and pepper to taste, and let them simmer slowly. Then have ready some small pieces of toast, raise the brains carefully and lay on the toast. Serve immediately.

PORK.

Some folks of long ago said that the devil went into the swine and never came out. Perhaps he did, but I like ham. So many other people like ham and pork too, and persist in eating them, that it is better to give recipes for cooking them well. Buy, if possible, pork from the pig that has been home raised. Many people are poisoned by not buying their pork with care. There is hardly any part of the pig but can be eaten, and consequently many people almost live upon it.

Pork Chops.

Buy loin chops, have pan very hot and keep frying until nicely browned. Serve immediately.

BOILED HAM.

Put a good sized ham into boiling water and keep it boiling for about four hours, until very tender. Then let it stand until the water cools. Take out, skin it and pepper well. Stick some cloves into it, lay it where it will keep cool and cut thin. It makes a good lunch dish.

DEVILED HAM.

Cut some cold boiled ham very fine, add a little good mustard and pepper. Take three hard boiled eggs, chop fine, put all into the bowl and mix well. Then put into a mold or deep dish, press hard and cut thin.

SPARE RIBS.

Wipe the spare ribs off well and salt and pepper to taste. Have your oven hot and bake the ribs one-half hour. Have the bones cracked before cooking. Bad for dyspeptics.

ROAST PORK.

Take about six or eight pounds of the ribs of fresh pork and slash the skin, if it is not removed. Salt and pepper well, sprinkle the whole with some flour and a little sage. Have the oven very hot and bake about two hours, taking care not to burn it. Pork requires more cooking than any other kind of meat as it is very unwholesome if not well cooked. Baste well, while roasting. Serve hot. Some always serve apple sauce with roast pork.

LIVER.

Liver of any kind is better soaked in water a little while before using. Then slice it, have ready a pan with good hot butter and brown the slices, taking care to let them cook through well as liver is not very digestible. Serve hot.

Kidney Stew.

Take as many kidneys as will be required and put on to boil for a few minutes with a little salt. Then take up and cut into small square pieces. Put a good lump of butter into a pan. Let it brown, then put the kidneys in with a little water over them and boil well until tender. Add about one-half glass of good wine and one tablespoonful of flour wet with water to thicken the stew. Salt and pepper to taste, place little pieces of toast on a platter and pour the stew over them, serving hot.

Ham and Eggs.

Cut the ham into thin slices and have the pan good and hot. Lay the slices into the pan and brown well. Care should be taken not to burn. Fry the eggs in the fat and serve on the slices of ham.

Soup Stock.

Take from four to eight pounds of lean beef, with the shin bone and some mutton and veal. Put over the fire in a large pot, or stock-kettle, cover with cold water and simmer slowly for at least four hours. Take two large onions, one turnip, one carrot and a little celery. Cut up and put all into the stock. Boil well for two hours. Care should be taken to skim well before putting in the vegetables. When well boiled, strain and set away to cool. When cold, remove all the fat and put the stock where it will keep cool, It will keep for several days. Any kind of soup can be made from this stock. When a large quantity of this stock is made, it is well to put it into several small jars. Only one of these will be required at a time and the film of grease which makes an air tight covering, can be left on the top of the others until ready to use them. The stock will keep better in this way.

BOUILLON.

Buy from four to eight pounds of beef from shoulder. Put over the fire early in the morning in cold water and simmer slowly for about four hours. Skim well, then add salt and pepper to taste. Add two onions, one carrot, one turnip and a little celery, cut into small pieces. Cook slowly for three hours more. Then strain and set away to cool. Remove the fat when cold. This will keep for several days.

OX TAIL SOUP.

Cut up one ox tail with about two pounds of lean beef, a knuckle of veal and some mutton bones. Put all into a soup pot. Cover with cold water and simmer slowly. Stir occasionally, and remove all scum. After simmering for about four hours, put in salt, pepper and one onion. Cook two hours longer, then strain and set in a cool place. When cold skim, and it will be ready to serve. The longer soup is cooked, the better it is.

RICE-TOMATO SOUP.

Take some of the soup stock and put into it one cup of tomatoes. Heat well, let it stand a little, then add one-half cup of rice. Cook one-half hour before serving. Season well with salt and pepper. Serve very hot.

BEEF TEA OR BROTH FOR INVALIDS.

Buy two pounds of meat from the round, cut it up fine,

put into a stone jar and let stand in boiling water. Put one cup of cold water into the jar, cover tightly and boil for about three hours or until the meat is white and all goodness extracted from it. Then season with salt.

Bean Soup.

Pick over one pint of beans, wash and soak in cold water over night. In the morning, put them on to boil, covering with water. Boil slowly, being careful not to let them burn. Add water, if necessary. When the beans are well done, rub them through a colander. Then add about one quart of sweet milk, butter the size of a walnut, salt and pepper to taste. Put in rice boiler just before serving. This will not keep long on account of the milk. It is very good if properly made.

Potato Soup.

Pare and boil three good sized potatoes. Add one onion. When well boiled, rub through a colander. Add a quart of boiling milk, one tablespoonful of butter, salt and pepper to taste. Put into rice boiler and cook about one and one-half hours before serving. Serve very hot.

Tomato Cream Soup.

Take one pint of stock, one-half onion and one can of tomatoes. Boil one-half hour. Pass through a seive and return to the fire. Add one quart of sweet milk. Salt and pepper to taste and add a little Worcestershire Sauce: Serve very hot.

Corn Soup—For twelve persons.

Take nine good ears of corn and twelve tomatoes. Cut the corn from the cobs, mix with the tomatoes. Add two quarts of water and boil one half hour, then let it stand and add one pint of milk and a piece of butter the size of an egg. Salt and pepper to taste. Just before serving put in a pinch of soda. Always serve soup hot.

MUTTON BROTH.

Buy about two pounds of lean mutton from the shoulder, cut into small pieces, put into cold water and cook very slowly. Skim well, as the grease of mutton is not good. Cook about three hours, then strain and add one-half cup of rice. Salt and pepper to taste. Boil until rice is done and serve hot. Some people like a little onion, but when made for invalids, the onion should be omitted.

CLAM CHOWDER.

Pare and cut into small pieces four or six good sized potatoes. Boil, mash and add twenty-four large clams with their juice. Have ready about two quarts of warm sweet milk. Add the milk and a good tablespoonful of butter. Pepper and salt. Put all into a double kettle and cook a few minutes.

CLAM SOUP.

Take twenty-five fresh clams and heat well in their liquor in a double kettle. Just before serving, add one quart of hot milk, pepper and salt to taste, a large piece of butter and favor slightly with onion, if desired.

OYSTER SOUP.

Get two dozen fresh oysters or one can of preserved oysters. Put into a rice boiler and heat; then skim carefully. Scald one quart of fresh milk and just before serving pour the oysters into the milk. Add one tablespoonful of good butter. Salt and pepper to taste.

Oyster Soup, No. 2.
MADE FROM FRESH OYSTERS.

Cook the oyster juice in a double kettle. Pepper and salt to taste. Scald one quart of fresh milk and add the oyster juice with a tablespoonful of good butter. Put the oysters in the soup-tureen without cooking add one-half cup of cracker crumbs rolled very fine. Now pour the liquid over the oysters and crackers and serve immediately. In this way the oysters will be deliciously tender.

Lentil Soup.

Soak a pint of lentils over night in cold water. About nine o'clock in the morning, put them on to cook, add more water and a little beef. Boil until very soft, then rub through a colander and add about one quart of sweet milk, one tablespoonful of butter and pepper and salt to taste. Cook in a rice boiler not to burn the milk. Serve very hot.

Mock Turtle Soup.

Scrape a calf's head clean, leaving on the skin. Soak over night. In the morning put it on in a soup kettle and boil slowly until the flesh falls from the bones. Take out the meat and put the liquid back on the stove. When well done, add about four quarts of stock, one quart of tomatoes, one tablespoonful of cinnamon, a little cloves and allspice and two teaspoonfuls of sugar Salt and pepper. Let this stand in a soup kettle, adding one-half cup of browned flour with a little water. Then let all come to a boil and when ready to serve, add some of the meat, cut into small pieces, one glass of sherry wine and the juice of two lemons. Toast and butter two slices of white bread. Remove the crust, cut into small pieces and drop into the soup. Very good, if properly made.

CHICKEN BROTH.

Cut one good sized, old chicken into pieces, put in the soup pot, cover with water and boil slowly for about three hours. Some chickens are much older than the poultry dealers say, and require more cooking. When tender, remove the bones, strain the soup, add about one-half cup of rice, then boil very slowly for another half hour so as to keep the rice whole. Add pepper and salt and serve.

For invalids this soup is good, but it is better not to add the rice, as many people are not fond of it, or it may not agree with them.

TURKEY SOUP.

A very delicious soup may be made out of the bones of the turkey after the meat is removed. Put them into a pot and cover with cold water; boil slowly, and when the broth begins to look like soup, open a can of sweet corn and pour it into the pot. Boil about one-half hour longer. Then let it stand. Add salt and pepper to taste. Boil up again and serve at once.

SALSIFY OR OYSTER PLANT SOUP.

Take two bunches of salsify, scrape, and cut into small pieces. Put on to boil and, when tender, rub through a colander. About twenty minutes before serving, add one quart of sweet milk, a little piece of butter the size of a walnut and salt and pepper to taste. Heat to boiling point and serve immediately.

FOWL.

TURKEY.

HOW TO CHOOSE A GOOD TURKEY.

Select a large hen turkey, weighing about eight or ten pounds. If its feet and legs are clean, not covered with scales, and the end of the breast bone soft, it is good. Kill two days before using.

ROAST TURKEY.

Remove the entrails, pick off all the small feathers and singe carefully, then wash and dry off with a clean towel. Salt the inside well and lay it in a large pan until ready to fill. To make the stuffing, break up fine one loaf of stale bread and soak in water or milk. When soaked, beat well with a spoon. Add a lump of butter the size of an egg. Salt and pepper to taste. Sprinkle a little sage, or any other spice which may be desired. Some people like a little flavor of onion. When the onion is used, chop it fine and brown in a spider with hot butter, before putting it into the stuffing. Stuff the turkey, and sew up the breast. Lay it in a large baking pan, put butter, flour, salt and pepper over it. Have oven very hot at first, that the pores may be closed at once. Brown well and baste very often. It will take about two hours to cook thoroughly. A larger one will require a longer time.

To Make the Gravy.

Boil the heart, gizzard, liver and neck in two quarts of water two hours; take them out, chop very fine, and put them back again; thicken with one spoonful of flour wet with cold water, and season with pepper and salt. Let this simmer one hour longer, and when you dish the turkey turn the drippings into the gravy. Boil up once and send to the table.

Boned Turkey.

Buy an old turkey weighing about eight pounds. Clean well, cut into pieces, put on to boil until the meat will drop from the bones. Then take out of the pot and pick out all the bones. Chop meat very fine. (Some people like it better in pieces.) Season well with salt and pepper. Take a pint or more of the liquor in which it has boiled, and add to the meat. Then put into deep dish and press down. Let it stand until cold, cut thin, and serve. Very nice luncheon or tea dish, if well cooked.

How To Select Good Chicken.

The signs of a good chicken are about the same as those of a young turkey. The legs and feet should be clean and the end of the breast-bone soft. The spurs should be loose and short. When old, the legs are rough, the spurs hard and firmly fixed, and the end of breast-bone hard. There are few creatures more tender than a young chicken and few more tough than an old fowl. Great care should be taken in selecting. Young chickens are best for cooking in many ways, but spring chickens are generally poor, unless well fed. By some, the yellow chickens are preferred, by others, the white.

CHICKEN.

SPLIT BACK CHICKENS.

Split two young chickens down the back and clean well, then lay them into a baking pan and put salt, pepper, flour, and pieces of butter over them. Have a good hot oven ready and put a little boiling water into the pan, around the chickens, but not over them. Then baste, and when brown, turn them over in the pan and baste again well. They will cook in about one-half hour. When done, take them up on a hot platter. Pour gravy over them and serve hot at once.

FRIED CHICKEN.

Buy two young chickens. Clean, wash and wipe well. Cut them into pieces; flour and lay aside until ready to fry. Heat some butter in a pan and when very hot, lay pieces of chicken in. Salt and pepper well. Brown one side, then turn over and brown the other. When thoroughly cooked, cover up and take from the fire. When ready to serve, place chickens on hot platter, put one tablespoonful of flour in pan from which the chickens have been removed. Mix well with the fat in the pan, then add one cup of good cream or milk, stirring well all the time. Pour this gravy over the chicken and serve hot.

CHICKEN FRICASSEE.

Clean a nice sized chicken well and cut into small pieces. Put into the pot, cover with cold water and cook slowly for about two hours. If the chicken is old, it will take longer. When tender, salt and pepper. Wet two tablespoonfuls of flour with a little cold water and stir gradually into the chicken. Remove from the fire for fear of burning. Serve on crackers laid into a platter, taking pieces up carefully not to break them. Serve hot.

Chicken Pie.

Cut a young chicken into small pieces and parboil a little. Then take it up, lay it in a deep dish, salt, pepper and pour the liquor in which it was parboiled, over the pieces. Sift two cups of flour, in which, rub one-half cup of butter. Add a good pinch of salt, two teaspoonfuls of baking powder and one cup of sweet milk. Mix this dough well, roll out and lay over the chicken. Put in a moderately hot oven and bake to a nice light brown. Serve hot.

GAME.

QUAIL.

Clean six quail carefully, slit up the back, and lay over them thin slices of salt pork, a little butter, pepper and salt. Have a good hot oven and lay the quail in a pan with a little hot water and flour. Bake about one hour, then lay toast on the platter, put the quail on top of the toast and serve very hot.

FRIED QUAIL.

Fried quail are very nice. Cut very young ones down the back and flour well. Have ready some butter in a pan very hot, and when the pieces are nicely browned, cover very close and let them stand for a few minutes. Some people prefer them broiled, but great care has to be taken in broiling not to let them burn.

BROILED QUAIL.

Have ready a good bed of coals and have broiler very hot. Butter the platter. Salt and pepper the quail. Broil the quail quickly and lay on hot platter. Serve immediately.

SIGNS BY WHICH YOU MAY KNOW YOUNG DUCKS.

When young and tender the joints in the legs will break by the weight of the duck. The windpipe will break by a very little presure. Young geese are known by the same signs and also by the fact that the wings will meet over the back.

Roast Duck.

Buy young ducks and prepare by getting all the pinfeathers off nicely and singeing well. Clean and soak in salt water over night, then dry well on a clean napkin. Flour, salt, pepper and lay in a baking pan. Have ready a good hot oven. Put a little hot water in the pan about the duck. Bake two hours. Some like them stuffed like a turkey.

A good stuffing may be prepared in this way: Take one loaf of stale bread and soak in water or milk. Have ready two onions chopped fine and brown them in butter. Mix onion with bread, salt and pepper. Salt the bird well and fill with the stuffing.

Tame Pigeon.

These beautiful birds are used for food, though they are sometimes very dry eating and good only for pot pie, fricassee and stew. Among the many varieties are those with ruffled, raised feathers around the neck. The most beautiful ones are the best to eat. Squabs are young pigeons. They are very tender, delicate, and good food for invalids, when broiled or stewed.

English Snipes.

Broil or stew them.

FISH.

SALMON.

HOW TO CHOOSE SALMON.

This noble fish is considered very choice and nutritious. It is somewhat high priced. Salmon have small heads and are quite thick in the shoulders. They weigh from six to twelve pounds. When cut, the flesh ought to be solid, flaky and pink.

BOILED SALMON.

Take about three pounds of salmon, wrap it in a clean cloth, put into a pan and cover with water. Salt it and boil for about one-half hour. Care must be taken in taking out, not to break it. Season with pepper, salt and cream.

FRIED SALMON.

Cut the salmon into thin slices, have a pan hot with some butter, and fry very slowly. Be careful not to let fat soak into the fish. Serve very hot. If any salmon is left cold, take potatoes and make fish cakes for breakfast. These are very good fried in butter. Cut fresh limes in quarters and serve with fish.

BAKED SHAD.

Buy a good young shad. Open down the middle, clean well and wipe dry. Then make stuffing of bread crumbs, a little butter, pepper and salt, sprinkling over it a little sage. Stuff the fish and lay in a deep pan, having ready a good hot oven. Bake one-half hour. Lay on platter and serve very hot.

Shad Fried.

Remove the back bone, cut with a sharp knife into thin pieces and have ready a hot pan, well buttered. Fry until brown.

Silver Smelt.

Take out the bones, flour the fish or put corn meal on them and have ready, butter in a good, hot pan. Fry the fish till nicely done. Salt, pepper and butter to taste. Serve hot.

Broiled Smelt.

Prepare in the same manner, and broil over hot coals, browning well on both sides. Lay on a hot platter. Salt, pepper, and butter to taste.

Fresh Mackerel.

Take out the back bone, wipe dry and broil over hot coals. Then butter, salt, pepper, and serve on a hot platter.

Salt Mackerel.

Soak the fish over night in cold water, changing water several times. Then in the morning, put the fish in the pan with boiling water and cook slowly for about ten minutes, then strain off the water and lay fish on platter, butter, pepper and serve hot.

Lake Trout Broiled.

These are very fine fish, either baked or broiled.

Clean trout well, slit down the back, have the fire good and hot. Broil the fish, browning well on both sides. Lay on a hot platter. Butter, pepper and salt. Serve very hot.

Lake Trout Fried.

Prepare as for broiling by rolling in corn meal, or bread crumbs. Have ready a pan with butter very hot and fry very quickly, so as not to soak fat. Serve very hot.

Cod Fish.

This is very good when fresh, cut into thin, (half inch) slices, and fried or broiled.

Salt Cod Fish.

Soak fish over night, removing all the bones. Boil some potatoes and put in with fish. Mash well and make into small cakes. Fry brown in very hot butter, and serve immediately.

SALADS.

CHICKEN SALAD.

Buy an old hen and boil well until the meat falls off from the bones. Then pick out all the white meat and some of the dark. Put into a bowl and chop fine. Salt and peppor well. Then take several good heads of lettuce, cut up fine, and mix with the chicken. Add salad dressing, not making it too thin. If prepared two hours or more before using, it is better put in a cold place. Serve in salad dish, garnished with lettuce leaves and hard boiled eggs. Some people prefer celery, and when used, it should be very tender.

SALAD DRESSING.

Beat the yolks of six eggs well. Then add one-half cup of vinegar, half a teaspoonful of salt and a little red pepper. Stir all these well, then add one pint of good cream. Mix thoroughly, pour into a rice boiler and steam until thick. Very good and wholesome. Many who cannot eat a salad with oil, can eat this.

SALAD DRESSING, NO. 2.

This kind will last for one meal only. Take the yolks of two eggs and beat well with a silver fork. Add salt to taste, a little red pepper, one tablespoonful of vinegar and olive oil until the eggs are well thickened, dropping the oil in slowly, beating all the time. Some like a little mustard also.

POTATO SALAD.

Cut up boiled potatoes into small pieces. Take about one-half a cup of vinegar and put into it a good sized piece of butter, one-half teaspoonful of salt and a little red pepper. Mix all well together. Let it cool and pour over the potatoes. Very nice dish.

TOMATO AND LETTUCE SALAD.

Peel tomatoes and cut into round pieces. Take lettuce leaves and lay on salad dish. Lay the slices of tomatoes on the lettuce leaves, and pour the dressing over, or serve the dressing in a separate dish.

SHRIMP SALAD.

Prepare the shrimps, taking care that there are no bits of shell left. Have ready some nice lettuce leaves wel drained; lay the leaves around the salad bowl, then put shrimps in the middle of the dish. Pour over the dressing just before serving.

CRAB SALAD.

Prepare like shrimp salad.

SANDWICHES.

HAM SANDWICHES, NO. 1.

Take two pounds of boiled ham and chop it very fine. Mix well with this, one teaspoonful of Durham mustard and one shake of cayenne pepper. Slice the bread thin, cut off all crust, and butter. Spread the ham between the slices and put together evenly.

HAM SANDWICHES, NO. 2.

Slice boiled ham very thin and lay it between the slices of bread prepared as in Ham Sandwiches, No 1. Veal, roast-beef, or tongue may be used in the same way.

COTTAGE CHEESE SANDWICHES.

Slice the bread thin, cut off all crust, and butter. Spread the slices with cottage cheese and put them together evenly.

BONED TURKEY SANDWICHES.

Lay the boned turkey between slices of bread prepared as for Cottage Cheese Sandwiches.

EGG SANDWICHES.

Slice hard boiled eggs, and season with salt and pepper. Prepare the bread as previously directed, and lay the sliced eggs between the slices.

VEGETABLES.

Vegetables should be very carefully cooked. Many people think that beans and beets are very indigestible. But this is not so, when well cooked. Young housekeepers are very apt to serve the vegetables before they are thoroughly done. Beware of this and give them plenty of time.

BOILED POTATOES.

Pare and wash well as many potatoes as may be necessary for dinner. About one-half hour before it is time to serve, lay them into a pan of boiling water and boil briskly. Some potatoes take longer to cook then others, but most of them will cook in one-half hour. When well done, salt, pour out the water and set on the back of the stove to dry. This will make them white and mealy.

SCALLOPED POTATOES.

Pare and slice ten potatoes. Take a deep dish and put into it a layer of potatoes, sprinkling over them, flour, salt, pepper and a little butter. Then put another layer of potatoes with seasoning as before. Keep on until the dish is full. Just before putting into the oven, add a pint of sweet milk. Bake about three-quarters of an hour in a slow oven. Good, if well done.

LYONNAISE POTATOES.

Cut twelve cold boiled potatoes into square pieces. Fry two teaspoonfuls of chopped onions in two tablespoonfuls of butter, then add potatoes, stirring with a fork, being careful not to break them. Salt and pepper to taste. Cook ten minutes longer. When done add parsley and serve hot.

CREAM POTATOES.

Cut four good sized potatoes into square pieces. Boil until tender, but not until they break. Then drain in hot colander and add one cup of good cream. If cream is not at hand, add one cup of milk and a little butter. Pepper and salt to taste. Chop up a little parsley and scatter over after putting in the dish. Serve hot.

BREAKFAST POTATOES.

Cut six good sized potatoes into small square pieces. Heat some butter in a pan until very hot. Put potatoes into the pan, then add a little more butter, salt and pepper. Cover well while cooking, being careful not to let them burn. Stir occasionally. When done, place in dish and serve hot.

BOILED SWEET POTATOES.

Sweet potatoes require more time for cooking than Irish potatoes. Take large, fine potatoes, wash, clean and boil with the skins on in plenty of water, but without salt. They will require at least one hour for cooking. Pour off the water, set them back on the stove in the pot in which they were cooked to dry for a few minutes. Peel them before sending to the table.

BAKED SWEET POTATOES.

Select those which are of nearly the same size, but not too large. Bake like common potatoes, except that they require a longer time.

BAKED SWEET POTATOES, No. 2.

Steam the potatoes until they are almost done. Then put them into the oven and bake until they are soft at the heart.

RICE AS A VEGETABLE.

Rice should first be picked over carefully, washed and dried. Then put into boiling water, salted and boiled twenty minutes. There should be plenty of water. At the end of twenty minutes, pour off the water, cover the rice and set it on the back of the stove to steam for about fifteen minutes. If it steams well during this time it will be done, and every grain will be distinct and whole. If any water is left, pour it off and for every cup of rice add one-half cup of milk. Warm the milk before adding it.

SQUASH.

Peel the squash, cut into pieces, put in steamer and cook one hour. When done, drain well and mash fine. Add salt, pepper and butter. Serve hot.

STUFFED SQUASH.

Pare a small squash and slice off the top. Take out the seeds and lay the squash in salt and water for a few minutes. Then take out, dry and fill with a good stuffing of crumbs, chopped salt pork, parsley etc., wet with gravy. Put on the top slice and set the squash in a pudding dish, with a few teaspoonfuls of melted butter and as much hot water. Cover and bake two hours. Then take out, lay in a fresh dish and pour the gravy over it.

TURNIPS.

Pare the turnips and cut into small pieces. Put them in water well salted and boil until tender. Then drain thoroughly. Mash fine, add a piece of butter, pepper and salt to taste and a small teaspoonful of sugar. Mix thoroughly and serve hot.

TURNIPS, NO. 2.

Pare and cut into square pieces. Put into boiling water and cook until done. Pour off the water, season with butter, salt and pepper.

BEETS.

Some people think this vegetable not fit for the table but it is very good, when properly cooked. Beets should cook at least four hours, keeping plenty of water on them. When tender, pour cold water over them and the skin will come off. Then put into a bowl and chop fine. Add salt, pepper, vinegar and a little butter. Place over fire again and serve hot.

BEETS, NO. 2.

Beets are always good for fresh pickle. Boil them well, skin, cut into thin slices, pour vinegar over them and serve cold.

BAKED TOMATOES.

Take as many tomatoes as necessary for dinner and bake them whole. Then scoop out a little place at the top of each one. Fill with cracker crumbs, a little salt, pepper and butter. Put them back into the oven to brown. Care must be taken not to burn them. Serve hot. Very nice.

Scalloped Tomatoes.

Boil some macaroni well. Place a layer of macaroni in an earthen dish, then a layer of tomatoes. Season well with pepper, salt and a little butter. Then another layer of macaroni and tomatoes seasoned as before and so on, making the last layer of tomatoes. Bake about twenty minutes in a moderately hot oven. Some like cracker or bread crumbs over the top. Serve hot.

Steamed Tomatoes.

Peel the tomatoes, cut into pieces and put into a pan. Granite ware is always the best, as tin or iron spoils the taste. Steam slowly for about one-half hour, then add a lump of butter the size of a walnut, a half teaspoonful of salt, pepper to taste and one teaspoonful of sugar. Have ready some pieces of toast and break into the tomatoes just before serving. For steaming, use the double granite ware kettles, if possible.

String Beans.

This vegetable should be cooked a long time. Two hours is not too long, but care should be taken not to let them burn. Break up into small pieces and put on to boil. If very old, they will require a pinch of baking soda in the water. Skim, and they will cook without changing the water. Take out when well done, strain off all the water, add salt and pepper to taste and a good sized piece of butter. Serve hot.

Lima Beans.

These beans are very good in summer. Shell and put on to boil. Take care to keep plenty of water on them. Cook about one hour. Salt and pepper. Add cream, or if there is no cream, a little butter.

Green Peas.

Green peas are very nice when fresh. Boil not more than one-half hour. When done, strain off the water, salt and pepper to taste and add a little butter or cream. Do not let them stand long after cooking. Serve very hot.

Corn Oysters.

Cut the kernels of six or eight good ears of corn from the cobs and put into an earthen bowl. Break two eggs on the corn. Add a little salt and pepper to taste and two tablespoonfuls of flour wet with water. Mix well. Have ready in a pan some butter very hot. Drop spoonfuls of the corn into the pan and fry brown. Very good.

Green Corn.

Take as many ears of corn as are needed for dinner. Pull off the husks and boil the ears about twenty minutes before they are to be served. Pour on boiling water and cover tightly. When done, take out of water and serve on platter, wrapped in clean napkin.

Asparagus

This vegetable is very nice when young and tender. Cut the hard part off the stalks and tie them up in nice little bunches. Boil about one-half hour. Season and have ready some slices of toast well buttered. Lay the asparagus on the toast and serve hot. Some like cream on asparagus, but if used, it should be poured on just before the asparagus is taken to the table.

Spinach.

Take the leaves of spinach, no stems, and wash them thoroughly. Put them in enough salt and water to cover them and boil until tender. Then take them out and put into cold water to set the fresh green color. Let them remain in the water until cold, then rub through a colander with a potato masher. Heat, season and serve.

Spinach, No. 2.

Wash the leaves well, taking care to pick out all poor ones. Put on over the stove in boiling water and cook about one-half hour. Then strain well. Chop up fine, add salt, pepper and a good piece of butter. Mold in little cups, as many as will be wanted for dinner. Set the cups in a pan of hot water and when ready to serve, turn out of the cups on a warm platter. Have ready some hard boiled eggs, cut them into slices and lay over each cup of spinach. It makes a very nice appetizing dish. Serve hot.

Egg Plant.

Peel the plant and cut into slices, salt well, cover over and let them lie for two hours or more. Drain off all the water and wipe the slices. Dip in butter and cracker crumbs. Have ready some butter in a hot pan, and fry rapidly, but take care not to burn. Serve very hot.

Egg Plant.
Spanish.

Put two large egg plants in a kettle of boiling water.

Boil one hour. Remove the pulp and mix with it half an onion chopped fine, one-half a green pepper, and salt to taste. Put all into an earthen dish, and pour over it half a cup of cream. Place in the oven and let it bake slowly one-half hour.

CAULIFLOWER.

Remove all the green leaves except a few of the little ones. Put on in boiling water and cook until tender, which will take about twenty minutes. Care should be taken not to break in cooking. Take up carefully, drain, salt, butter and serve hot. Instead of butter, cream may be used.

STEWED CELERY.

Clean the heads of celery thoroughly. Take off coarse, green outer leaves, cut into small pieces and stew in a little broth. When tender, add some rich cream, a little flour and a little butter. Season with pepper and salt.

MUSHROOMS.

Take off the outside of the mushrooms and put them into a pan with a little boiling water. Boil about one-half hour, then add salt, pepper and butter. Serve hot in a deep platter. Mushrooms are of a bright pink inside, while toadstools are white or yellow. Another method of distinguishing between mushrooms and toadstools is by putting in a silver spoon when cooking. If poison the spoon will be blackened.

FRIED MUSHROOMS.

Wash and pare them, cut off the stems, have ready a very hot pan with butter, and fry until thoroughly done.

Succotash.

Take ten ears of good corn and one pint of Lima beans. Cut the corn from the cobs and stew gently with the beans until tender, using as little water as possible. Season with butter or cream. Salt and pepper. Very rich and nourishing dish, invented by the Indians.

Succotash, No. 2.

Boil one quart of Lima or string beans until tender, then cut the grains from ten ears of corn and scrape the cobs. Drain the water from the beans, add the corn and season with salt, pepper, and a good sized piece of butter. If too dry, add a little cream. Cook two minutes after adding the corn.

ENTREES.

DEVILED CRAB.

Boil six crabs and chop the meat. Add three tablespoonfuls of stale bread crumbs, one-half glass of good cream, yolks of three boiled eggs chopped, one tablespoonful of butter and pepper and salt to taste. Mix all together and put back into the shells. Sprinkle the top with cracker crumbs and a little butter and brown in a quick oven. Serve hot in the shells.

FISH CROQUETTES.

Chop one pint of cold boiled fish, free from the bones and skin. Add one pint of hot mashed potatoes. Mix well. Season with butter, pepper and salt. Bake slowly for one-half hour, then serve hot.

CHICKEN CROQUETTES.

Take the meat from one boiled chicken, one ounce of melted butter, one ounce of sifted flour, one cup of the liquor in which the fowl was boiled, one cup of cream, pepper and salt to taste, two eggs and a little nutmeg. Boil butter, flour, cream and a little water together for two minutes, then mix with the chicken. Cool and shap into balls. Dip them into beaten eggs and then roll them lightly in cracker crumbs and fry brown.

SCALLOPED OYSTERS.

Drain one quart of large oysters in a colander. Then take an earthen dish, put in a layer of cracker crumbs, then a layer of oysters, pepper, salt and butter. Continue until the dish is full, putting a layer of crackers on the top. Set in a good hot oven and bake about twenty minutes until it is a nice brown. Serve hot.

FRIED OYSTERS.

Drain liquor from large oysters. Have ready cracker crumbs and one egg well beaten. Dip the oysters into the eggs, then into the cracker crumbs. Have a pan hot with some butter and fry very rapidly until done. Lay upon a hot platter.

BROILED OYSTERS.

Take as many oysters as are required and have ready a good bed of hot coals. Drain the oysters well, lay them on the gridiron and hold over the coals. Great care should be taken not to burn them. Have ready small slices of toast well buttered; lay the oysters on the toast and serve hot. A very nice dish, but very difficult to cook without scorching.

STUFFED POTATOES.

Select potatoes all of one size, cut off each end and bake. Take from the oven and scoop out the inside with a spoon, being careful not to break the skins. Add to the part scooped out, butter, pepper and salt, beating together until very light. Then fill the skins, lay on a buttered pan and set in the oven until brown on top. Very nice.

Corn Fritters.

Take one pint of green corn grated, one-half teacup of milk, one-half teacup of sifted flour, one teaspoonful of baking powder, one tablespoonful of melted butted, two eggs and salt and pepper to taste. Stir well, fry in butter and serve hot.

Pilaf.

A Russian Dish.

Pick over carefully one cup of rice, but do not wash it. Add one tablespoonful of butter and beat them together. Then pour over one pint of boiling mutton broth. Stir well once only, then set on the back of the stove and cook slowly for one hour. Serve as a vegetable.

JEWELRY  HOSIERY

RIBBONS,

KID GLOVES,

"CHEAPEST PLACE IN TOWN."

39 EAST SANTA CLARA STREET.

LADIES', CHILDREN'S, INFANTS',

FURNISHING ✷ GOODS.

CORSETS   STATIONERY.   BRUSHES

⁕WOMEN ✲ PHYSICIANS.⁕

San Jose is rich in Women Doctors. For a long while they numbered seven, but now a slightly profane person has dubbed them "The Sacred Nine." Lately the coming here of a Lady Dentist brings the medical women up to a half score. May "Lizzie's Cook Book" be helpful to them and their patients.

DR. E. S. MEADE,

OFFICE AND RESIDENCE—33 North Third Street,

✢ SAN JOSE, CAL. ✢

OFFICE HOURS—10 a. m. to 12 m., and 4 to 5 p. m.   TELEPHONE 68.

MISS C. A. GOSS, M. D.,

HOMEOPATHIC PHYSICIAN,

96 North Third St., - San Jose, Cal.

OFFICE HOURS—1 to 3 p. m.; 6 to 7 p. m.

E. R. OSBORN, M. D.

PHYSICIAN AND SURGEON,

OFFICE AND RESIDENCE—68 South Third St., San Jose, Cal.

OFFICE HOURS—10 to 12 m., and 2 to 4 p. m.

DR. SARA BROWN BAILEY,

The Richmond Building, - 59 South Second Street,

✢ SAN JOSE, CAL. ✢

OFFICE HOURS—10 to 12 m., and 2 to 4 p. m.

DR. ALIDA CORNELIA AVERY,

Formerly of Denver, and for nine years ('65–'74) Resident Physician at Vassar College, Poughkeepsie, N. Y.

Seventh and Santa Clara Streets, - - SAN JOSE, CAL.

OFFICE HOURS—10 to 12 m., and 2 to 4 p. m.

PICKLES.

CHOW-CHOW.

Chop one peck of green tomatoes, twelve onions, three small heads of good cabbage, three red peppers and spinkle well with salt. Put all into a coarse bag and drain over night. In the morning, put into the preserving kettle with two pounds of brown sugar, one-half a cup of grated horseradish, two tablespoonfuls of black pepper, one tablespoonful of mustard, one teaspoonful of celery seed, some cloves and one teaspoonful of allspice. Cover the whole with good vinegar and boil until clear. Very nice.

PICKLED PEACHES.

Take about twenty pounds of good peaches and rub the skin well to get off all the down. Then lay the peaches in a large stone jar. Take one quart of good vinegar, three pints of brown sugar, boil, skim and pour over the peaches. Next morning pour off the syrup, heat it and pour on fruit again. This must be done for three successive mornings. Then drain off the syrup and sprinkle the top of the fruit with bits of whole cinnamon and whole cloves. Boil down the syrup until it is thick like molasses, pour boiling over the fruit, taking care to have enough to cover the peaches well. Put into a jar, let it cool and cover closely.

PICKLED PEACHES, NO. 2.

Take twenty pounds of peaches, peel carefully and cut

in halves. Have ready a syrup of two quarts of good vinegar, two pounds of brown sugar, one tablespoonful of cloves, one of cinnamon and one of allspice. Boil the syrup. Then drop in the peaches and boil up, but not so that the peaches will break. Put into glass jars.

Sweet Pickles.

Take about five hundred small cucumbers, three quarts of good vinegar, three pounds of brown sugar, one ounce of allspice and one of cloves and of cinnamon and a few small red peppers. Let the cucumbers stand all night in salt water. Then drain and put on to boil in vinegar and sugar. Boil gently for about five minutes. Then put in pepper and seasoning. Put in jars.

Tomato Sauce.

Cook tomatoes until soft and rub through a colander. Boil six hours, stirring often. When done, pour into a stone jar and cool. Then add one pint of good vinegar, bottle, seal tight and put in a cool place.

Tomato Catsup.

Take one pint of ripe tomatoes, cut out stem ends and put in a preserving kettle. Add one tablespoonful of salt, pepper, cloves and celery, one teaspoonful of cayenne pepper, two teaspoonfuls of ground mustard and one pint of vinegar. Pour into a kettle boil and skim. When done bottle and seal.

Chili Sauce.

Take fifty ripe tomatoes, twenty onions and two bunches of celery. Chop very fine and add one gill of good vinegar, three pounds of good brown sugar, one tablespoonful each of powdered Chili, allspice, cloves, cinnamon and salt. Boil two hours. Then bottle and seal.

PUDDINGS.

SNOW PUDDING.

Dissolve one-half a box of gelatine in one pint of cold water. When soft add one pint of boiling water, the juice and rind of two lemons and two cups of sugar, strain and let stand until cold. Then beat well the whites of three eggs and add them to the gelatine, beating all well together. Pour into molds and set on ice.

CUSTARD FOR SNOW PUDDING.

Eggs, ... 3.
Milk, ... 1 pint.
Sugar, ... 2 tablespoonfuls.

Beat the yolks of three eggs well, add a pint of milk and two tablespoonfuls of sugar. Then beat all well together, put in the rice boiler and cook until done. Set away to cool. When cold, pour over snow pudding.

SNOW PUDDING, No. 2.

Stir three heaping tablespoonfuls of corn starch into one pint of boiling water and boil fifteen minutes. Beat up the whites of three eggs and add three tablespoonfuls of sugar. Beat this into the corn starch after taking it from the fire and flavor with lemon. Let it cool, then pour over it a custard made like custard of number one. Flavor with vanilla.

Poor Man's Rice Pudding.

Put into an earthen dish two quarts of milk, one-half cup of rice, three tablespoonfuls of sugar and a little piece of butter. Mix well and bake in a slow oven, two hours or longer stirring occasionally not to let burn on top. When nearly done, grate little nutmeg over it. Serve cold.

Queen of Puddings.

Take one pint of stale bread crumbs and pour over them one pint of warm milk. Beat together the yolks of three eggs, two tablespoonfuls of sugar and one pint of cold milk. Stir well and add this to the bread already soaked. Put into an earthen dish, bake in a slow oven and stir occasionally until done. When done beat the whites of the three eggs and one tablespoonful of sugar together. Spread over the top of the pudding some good jelly and lay over this the whites of the eggs. Set in a hot oven until a light brown, being careful not to let it burn. Serve cold.

Apple Whip.

Apples, (good, large and ripe), ... 2
Sugar, ... 1 cup.
Eggs, ... 2.

Grate the apples, adding sugar while grating to keep apples from turning black. Then stir in the beaten whites of the eggs, beating all well for a half hour. Put into a glass dish and set in a cool place.

Serve with this a custard made as follows: Beat the yolks of two eggs with a tablespoonful of sugar. Put a pint of milk into a rice boiler, heat it, pour in eggs and sugar and let it thicken. Enough for four people.

Lemon Meringue.

Put into a pint of boiling water, a lump of butter the size of a walnut. Mix two tablespoonfuls of corn starch with a little cold water. Stir this into the boiling water until thick. Then take the juice of two lemons and one lime and one cup of sugar. Add to the corn starch the beaten yolks of three eggs, then the fruit juice and sugar and put all in an earthen dish. Beat the whites of the three eggs, spread over the top and set in the oven until it is brown. Take care not to burn. Set away to cool.

Floating Island.

Take one quart of good milk, the yolks of six eggs well beaten, a pinch of salt and two tablespoonfuls of sugar. Beat all well together and put in rice boiler. Cook slowly. When done add about three drops of vanilla. Pour the custard in a glass dish. Then beat the whites of the eggs well with two tablespoonfuls of sugar and drop into the custaad with a spoon. Set on ice to cool. Serve with sponge cake.

Fruit Tapioca.

Tapioca,	1 cup.
Boiling water,	1 pint.
Sugar,	½ cup.

Take one cup of tapioca, soak over night, put it into a rice boiler with one pint of boiling water and one-half cup of sugar. Cook until clear. Then add apricots, peaches or apples. Stir well, put in a glass dish to cool and serve with cream.

Bavarian Cream.

Take one-half a cup of gelatine and soak in cold

water about one-half hour. Warm a pint of good rich milk in a rice boiler and put the gelatine in the milk when warmed. Beat the yolks of two eggs with a tablespoonful of sugar. Add this to the milk and steam until it becomes like custard. Remove from the fire and set away to cool. Then whip one pint of good cream well and beat up the whites of the eggs, one tablespoonful of sugar and a little vanilla. Add this to the custard. Then put all into a glass dish and set to cool. If made early in the morning it will be ready in about five hours.

Steamed Rice

Milk,	1 quart.
Rice,	2/3 of a cup.
Salt,	1 pinch.

Mix well together one quart of sweet milk, two-thirds of a cup of rice and a good pinch of salt. Put into a mold and set in a steamer. Steam until the rice is like jelly. When cold turn out of the mold and serve with sugar and cream.

Coffee Jelly.

Gelatine,	1/2 box.
Strong coffee,	1 pint.
Sugar,	1 cup.
Boiling water	1 pint.

Soak one-half box of gelatine for half an hour in cold water. Pour the coffee over the gelatine, stir in the sugar and add boiling water. Strain through clean linen into a mold and cool. Serve with whipped cream.

Rhubarb Pudding.

Peel two bunches of rhubarb and cut into small pieces. Put a layer of rhubarb in an earthen dish, add sugar and a little butter. Then a layer of bread crumbs, (brown or white are equally good), then a layer of rhubarb with sugar and butter and so on until the dish is full. Put the bread crumbs on top, cover and cook in a slow oven for about two hours. Ten or fifteen minutes before removing it from the oven, take off the cover, that the pudding may brown nicely. Serve cold.

Baked Custard.

Milk, ... 1 quart.
Eggs, ... 4
Sugar, ... 3 tablespoonfuls.

Beat the eggs and add the milk. Then stir in the sugar and beat all well together. Put into cups, set in a pan of hot water and bake in a moderate oven. Grate a little nutmeg over the top and serve cold.

Souffle Pudding.

Milk, ... 1 quart.
Sifted flour, ... ½ cup.
Eggs, ... 4.
Sugar, ... 3 tablespoonfuls.

To one quart of milk when boiling, add one-half cup of sifted flour, stirring well all the time until thick. Add the beaten yolks of four eggs and three tablespoonfuls of sugar. Stir well into the milk and set to cool. When cold, half an hour before serving, beat the whites of the eggs and add to the mixture. Bake in a buttered dish in a moderate oven for twenty minutes. Serve immediately.

COTTAGE PUDDING.

Milk,	1 cup.
Sugar,	½ cup.
Melted butter,	2 tablespoonfuls.
Baking powder,	1 teaspoonful.
Eggs,	2.

Sift the baking powder into a pint of flour. Mix all well together. Bake half an hour and serve with a liquid sauce.

GOOD FRUIT PUDDING.

Stoned raisins,	2 pounds.
Currants,	1 pound.
Citron,	½ pound.
Chopped suet,	½ pound.
Stale bread crumbs,	2 pounds.
Eggs,	6.
Sour milk,	½ cup.
Soda,	1 teaspoonful.
Molasses,	1 cup.
Brown sugar,	2 cups.
Flour,	1 cup.
Cinnamon,	½ teaspoonful.
Cloves,	½ "
Allspice,	½ "
Nutmeg,	1.

Mix the molasses, sugar and eggs all well together; then add the sour milk, having first dissolved the soda in it. Add the bread crumbs. Stir all of these well together. Have the fruit well floured. Add suet first, then the fruit, and stir all thoroughly. Then add one cup of flour, one-half teaspoonful of cinnamon, the same of cloves, of allspice and of grated nutmeg. Have the two quart pail well greased, pour the batter into it, cover tightly and steam four hours. This will keep for several weeks and can be re-warmed when wanted.

Strawberry Short-Cake.

Rub one cup of butter into one pint of flour, add one teaspoonful of salt, two teaspoonfuls of baking powder and one cup of sweet milk. Mix up but not too stiff. Roll out and bake in jelly tins. Spread the berries, well sugared, between the layers. Serve hot.

Sweet Short-Cake.

Beat a lump of butter the size of an egg to a cream. Add one cup of sugar, two eggs, the whites and yolks beaten separately, one cup of sweet milk, two teaspoonfuls of baking powder and flour enough to make a stiff batter. Bake in jelly tins. Mash and sugar strawberries and spread between the layers, putting whole berries on the top. Sprinkle with sugar.

Suet Pudding.

Molasses	½ cup.
Eggs	2
Milk	1 cup
Chopped suet	½ cup
Salt	1 teaspoonful
Baking powder	2 teaspoonfuls
Sifted flour	3 small cups
Raisins	2 cups, (or one of any kind of fruit.)

Mix all well together, season with a little cinnamon and nutmeg and steam three hours.

Sauce for this pudding.—Beat up one-half cup of butter, two cups of sugar and a little boiled water and season with nutmeg. Beat them well together.

ICE CREAM.

Eggs	3
Good cream	1 quart
Milk	1 quart
Sugar	½ cup

Beat the milk, eggs and sugar well together, then put on in the rice boiler and cook until like custard. Set away to cool. When cold add one quart of good cream, one cup of sugar and vanilla or any other flavoring according to taste. Freeze.

ICE CREAM, NO. 2.

Take as many quarts of good sweet cream as will be required. Add one cup of sugar for every quart of cream and a little vanilla or any other kind of flavoring. Put into freezer and freeze for about ten minutes. Pack well until used.

FRUIT CREAM.

Sugar	2 large cups.
Milk	1 pint
Eggs	2
Gelatine	2 tablespoonfuls
Cream	1 quart
Fruit	—

Soak the gelatine half an hour. Beat the eggs well, then beat the eggs, sugar, milk and gelatine together. Put this into the rice boiler, cook until like custard, then let it cool. When cold, add one quart of good cream and peaches or any other kind of fruit. Rub fruit through a sieve. Mix all well together. Freeze.

STRAWBERRY CREAM.

Mash well one quart of good fresh strawberries with one cup of sugar and rub through a sieve. Dissolve two tablespoonfuls of gelatine in cold water, then add to the gelatine one pint of warm milk. Stir well until the gelatine is dissolved. Then add berries and one pint of whipped cream.

Strawberry Cream, No. 2.

Rub one quart of strawberries through a sieve and mix with three pints of rich cream whipped to a froth. Add one ounce of dissolved gelatine. Put into glasses and set on ice. Serve in the glasses.

Lemon Ice.

Soak two tablespoonfuls of gelatine in cold water, then add one quart of boiling water, juice of two lemons and two cups of sugar. Put the rind of one lemon in for a few minutes. Strain all and when cool put in the freezer and freeze well.

Junket.

Warm one quart of milk slightly and add two tablespoonfuls of sugar and three tablespoonfuls of liquid rennet. Mix well, put into a glass dish and set on ice. Good for invalids.

Chocolate Ice Cream.

Cream	1 quart
Milk	1 quart
Sugar	2 cups
Eggs	2
Grated chocolate	5 tablespoonfuls

Beat the eggs well and rub the chocolate smooth with a little milk. Then mix all and heat to nearly boiling point, stirring all the time. When cold beat in one quart of good cream and freeze.

Frozen Peaches.

Peeled peaches,	2 quarts.
Sugar,	1 pound.
Water,	1 quart.

Put the sugar over the peaches and let them stand two hours. Then mash fine, add the cold water and freeze.

Tapioca Ice.

Soak one cup of tapioca over night. In the morning put it on to boil. Add one cup of sugar and boil until clear. Chop up one pineapple and pour the tapioca over it. Stir well and put into a mold. When cold serve with cream and sugar.

EGGS.

HOW TO TELL FRESH EGGS.

If eggs are put into a bowl of cold water the fresh ones will float to the top. One of the best ways to be sure of fresh eggs, however, is to buy them of a dealer who has them brought in fresh every day.

JELLIED EGGS.

Pour a quart of boiling water in a dish, lay as many eggs into it as the water will cover, ten minutes before serving, cover tight. Very good, especially for invalids.

BAKED EGGS.

Lay the eggs in a pan and bake for one-half hour in a moderately hot oven. This cooks both whites and yolks until mealy like a baked potato. Invalids can often eat eggs baked in this way, when they cannot eat them boiled soft or poached.

BAKED EGGS, NO. 2.

Put a lump of butter in a baking pan and let it melt, then break eggs into it and set in a moderately hot oven. Watch carefully that they do not burn. Bake from eight to ten minutes.

SCRAMBLED EGGS.

Take a dozen half sheets of stiff note paper and turn up the edges of each piece, making little dishes. Break the eggs in a saucer. Place the dishes on the top of a moderately hot stove, put a little butter in each one and grease the whole surface carefully. Drop an egg into each dish and stir gently with a silver fork. Season with a little pepper and salt. Serve hot. Very delicate and nice, but difficult to cook well.

Scrambled Eggs, No. 2.

Heat a pan on top of the stove with a little butter in it. Break eggs in a dish and then put into the pan. Season well and stir until done. When cooked enough, the eggs will be light. Take up on a hot platter.

Poached Eggs.

Pour boiling water into pan and add a pinch of salt. Break eggs in a saucer one by one and drop into the water. Boil slowly, taking care to have the water cover the yolks. Have ready some pieces of bread well browned. Take each egg up carefully without breaking and lay on the toast.

Fried Eggs.

Have a hot pan with some butter in it. Break eggs in a saucer, drop into the pan and fry rapidly. Take out as soon as cooked, unless they are to be turned over. If they are to be turned, turn quickly. Then serve on a hot platter, on toast or on crackers dipped in boiling water.

Omelet.

Beat yolks and whites of six eggs separately. Into the yolks stir a pint of good milk and a little salt; then add the whites of the eggs, beating all together. Have ready a pan with very hot butter, pour in the eggs and set in a very hot oven. Bake for about eight minutes, watching to keep from burning. Take the omelet up carefully and lay on a hot platter, folding over on itself. Serve immediately.

HAM OMELET.

Make in the same manner as above and add one-half cup of boiled ham, chopped very fine. Take up on hot platter and fold as above.

OYSTER OMELET.

Make as in the first omelet, adding twelve fresh oysters chopped.

OMELET WITH JELLY.

Make omelet as in first recipe, then take it from the oven and spread it with one layer of currant or any acid jelly. Fold over as in the first.

CAKES.

"They cannot be too sweet for my lord's tartness."—*Shakespeare.*

ANGEL FOOD.

Granulated sugar,	1½ gills.
Flour,	1 gill.
Cream of tartar,	1 teaspoonful.
Eggs (whites only)	11.

Sift sugar five times. Sift flour and cream of tartar five times. Beat the whites of the eggs to a stiff froth and add the sugar. Then add flour and stir lightly until all is well mixed. Flavor with two drops of pure extract of almond. Have ready a tin pan that has never been greased, warm it well, put in the dough and bake in a slow oven for about thirty minutes. Take from the oven, turn pan bottom side up without removing cake and let it cool.

DELICATE CAKE.

Sugar,	1½ cups.
Butter,	½ "
Sweet milk,	1 "
Sifted flour,	2 "
Corn starch,	½ "
Baking powder,	2 teaspoonfuls.
Eggs (whites only,)	7.

Beat sugar and butter to a cream. Add milk and flour

sifted with baking powder, corn starch, and lastly the whites of the eggs well beaten before they are added. Flavor with vanilla. Pour into square baking pans and bake in a moderate oven about forty minutes.

Cocoanut Cake.

Sugar	2 cups
Sweet milk	1 cup
Flour	3 cups
Butter	2 tablespoonfuls
Eggs	3
Baking powder	2 teaspoonfuls

Beat sugar and butter to a cream, then add the eggs well beaten, and, last, the flour with baking powder. Bake in jelly-cake tins in quick oven.

Filling for this cake:

Eggs (whites only)	2
Powdered sugar	1 cup
Grated cocoanut	1 cup

Beat eggs well then add sugar and cocoanut. Spread between the layers and on the top of the cake.

Hickory Nut Cake.

Sugar	1½ cups.
Butter	¾ of a cup.
Sweet milk	1 cup.
Sifted flour	3 cups.
Chopped nuts	1 cup.
Baking powder	2 teaspoonfuls.

Beat butter and sugar to a cream. Mix all well together and bake in loaf.

Silver Cake.

Sugar	2 cups
Butter	½ cup
Sweet milk	1 cup
Sifted flour	3 cups
Eggs (whites only)	6
Baking powder	2 teaspoonfuls

Beat butter and sugar to a cream, then add milk, flour sifted with baking powder and whites of eggs well beaten first. Mix thoroughly, pour into square pans and bake in a slow oven.

Gold Cake.

Sugar	2 cups
Butter	½ cup
Sweet milk	½ cup
Sifted flour	2 cups
Eggs (yolks only)	5
Baking powder	2 teaspoonfuls

Mix and bake as in the recipe above.

1-2-3-4 Cake.

Butter	1 cup
Sugar	2 cups
Sifted flour	3 cups
Eggs	4
Baking powder	2 teaspoonfuls

Mix thoroughly, beat well and bake in a moderate oven.

Orange Cake.

Sugar	2 cups
Butter	½ cup

Sweet milk,	1 cup.
Sifted flour,	3 "
Eggs,	3.
Baking powder,	2 teaspoonfuls.

Beat butter and sugar to a cream. Add next the well beaten eggs, then the milk and last the flour and baking powder sifted together. Bake in sheets in moderate oven.

Filling for this cake:

Pulverized sugar,	2 cups.
Eggs (whites only),	2.
Juice and grated rind of one orange.	
Juice of one-half lemon.	

Beat all well together and spread between the layers and on the top.

Jelly Cake.

Sugar,	2 cups.
Milk,	1 cup.
Sifted flour,	3 cups.
Eggs,	3.
Butter,	2 tablespoonfuls.
Baking powder,	2 teaspoonfuls.

Beat butter and sugar to a cream then add eggs well beaten, milk, and flour sifted with baking powder. Bake in jelly cake tins. Spread good sour jelly between the layers as soon as taken from the oven.

Marble Cake.

white part.

Butter,	½ cup.
Sugar,	2 "

Sifted flour,	2½ cups.
Baking powder,	2 teaspoonfuls.
Eggs (whites only),	4.

Beat all well together.

DARK PART.

Butter,	½ cup.
Brown sugar,	1 "
Sour milk,	½ "
Sifted flour,	2 "
Eggs (yolks only),	4.
Soda,	1 teaspoonful.

A pinch of allspice, cloves and cinnamon each.

Put the soda into the sour milk and then beat all well together. Butter the pan well, pour in first a layer of the dark. Have the top layer dark, then the light and so continue until all is in the pan.
Bake in a slow oven about one hour.

MOLASSES CAKE.

Molasses,	1 cup.
Brown sugar,	1 "
Butter,	½ "
Strong coffee,	1 "
Sifted flour,	3 "
Soda,	1 teaspoonful.
Eggs,	2.

Dissolve soda in a little water then mix all thoroughly. Bake in thick sheets in a slow oven.

CREAM PUFFS.

Butter,	2 tablespoonfuls.
Sifted flour,	2 cups.
Eggs,	9.
Boiling water,	1 pint.

Put the butter in the boiling water then add the flour gradually, beating well until thick. When cool add the yolks of the eggs, beating with the hand, then the beaten whites. Have ready hot gem pans, pour in the dough and bake in a hot oven. When cold, open and fill with whipped or cooked cream.

FIG CAKE.

Eggs, ... 3.
Sugar, ... 1½ cups.
Butter, ... ½ cup.
Sweet milk, ... 1 "
Sifted flour, ... 3 cups.
Baking powder, ... 2 teaspoonfuls.

Mix thoroughly and bake in jelly cake tins.

FILLING FOR THIS CAKE.

Figs or raisins chopped very fine, ... 1 cup.
Walnuts, ... 1 cup.
Powdered sugar, ... 1½ cups.
Eggs (whites only,) .... 2.

Beat all well together and spread between the layers and on the top.

WEDDING CAKE.

Sugar, ... 2 cups.
Butter, ... 1 small cup.
Sweet milk, ... 1 cup.
Sifted flour, ... 3 cups.
Corn starch, ... ½ cup.
Baking powder, ... 2 teaspoonfuls.
Eggs (whites only,) .... 10.
Citron cut in small pieces, ... ½ cup.

Cream the butter and sugar, then add milk and flour

sifted with the baking powder and the corn starch. Beat the whites of the eggs well and stir in slowly. Then add the citron dusted with flour. Bake in moderately hot oven for about one hour.

Genuine Fruit Cake.

Butter,	1 cup.
Brown sugar,	2 cups.
Molasses,	1 cup.
Eggs,	8.
Sifted flour,	1 pound.
Soda,	1 teaspoonful.
Brandy,	1 wine glass.
Currants,	1 pound.
Stoned raisins,	1 "
Citron (cut fine,)	½ "
Blanched almonds,	1 cup.
Cinnamon,	1 teaspoonful.
Cloves,	1 "
Allspice,	1 "
Grated nutmeg,	1 "

Beat well together the butter, sugar and molasses. Then add the yolks of the eggs, the flour, the soda dissolved in a little water, and the brandy. Beat well, then add the fruit and spices. Mix all thoroughly and let it stand over night. In the morning beat the whites of the eggs and stir into the mixture. Put into well greased pans and bake three hours in a slow oven. Before taking from the oven, try with a broom splint. This will keep for years if not eaten but it generally is.

Cookies.

Sugar	2 cups
Butter	½ cup

CAKES.

Milk	1 cup
Flour	3 cups
Eggs	3
Baking powder	2 teaspoonfuls

Mix well, roll out thin, cut, sprinkle with sugar and bake in a good hot oven. Keep in a dry place.

Molasses Cookies.

Molasses,	1 cup.
Brown sugar,	1 "
Butter,	½ cup.
Flour,	3 cups.
Eggs,	2.
Soda,	1 teaspoonful.
Sour milk,	1 cup.

Dissolve soda in a little water, mix all well together, roll out thin, and bake in hot oven.

Black Cake.

Brown sugar	2 cups
Butter	1 cup
Flour (browned)	3 cups
Sweet milk,	1 cup.
Strong Coffee,	1 "
Eggs,	6.
Molasses,	2 tablespoonfuls.
Soda,	1 teaspoonful.
Cream of tartar,	2 "
Cinnamon,	1 "
Cloves,	1 "
Raisins,	2 lbs.
Currants,	1 "
Citron,	½ "

Beat butter and sugar together, add the eggs well beaten, the cup of sweet milk and the soda dissolved in a tablespoonful of water. Then put in the coffee and the flour in which the cream of tartar is sifted; lastly the fruit and spices and then mix all thoroughly and bake three hours in slow oven.

WATER MELON CAKE.

WHITE PART.

Sugar,..2 cups.
Butter,...1 "
Sweet milk,......................................1 "
Sifted flour,....................................3 cups.
Corn starch,.....................................½ cup.
Cream of tartar,................2 teaspoonfuls.
Soda,.................................1 teaspoonful.
Eggs (whites only,)..............................6.

Beat the whites of the eggs well, dissolve soda in a little water, then mix all thoroughly.

RED PART.

Red sugar, ...1 cup.
Butter,..½ "
Sweet milk,......................................1 "
Eggs (whites only,)..............................3.
Cream of tartar,................1 teaspoonful.
Soda,..½ "
Stoneless raisins,.............................1 cup.
Sifted flour,...................................2 cups.

Beat eggs, dissolve soda in a little water, then mix all thoroughly. Bake in a pan with a tube, taking care to keep the red part around tube and the white around the edge. It is well to have two people fill the pan together. Bake in a slow oven for nearly one hour.

White Sponge Cake.

Eggs (whites only,)..........................10.
Pulverized sugar,...................1½ tumblers.
Sifted flour,.............................1 tumbler.
Cream of tartar, ...1 teaspoonful.

Beat eggs to a stiff froth. Stir in sugar and flour lightly, having first sifted both twice. Flavor with vanilla or rose. Bake in moderately hot oven.

Plain Sponge Cake.

Pulverized sugar,..........................2 cups.
Eggs, ...6.
Sifted flour,.................................2 cups.
Baking powder....................1 teaspoonful.

Beat yolks of eggs with sugar. Add the flour and baking powder, then the beaten whites of the eggs. Stir all slowly until the top is covered with little bubbles. Bake in a moderately hot oven.

Pound Cake.

Sugar,..................................1 lb.
Sifted flour,............................1 lb.
Butter,......................1 lb. (scant.)
Eggs,....................................8.
Baking powder,..........2 teaspoonfuls.

Cream butter and sugar together thoroughly *with the hand*; add to this the beaten yolks and stir in well; next put in the sifted flour and powder and, last, the beaten whites. Pour into a square pan and bake one hour in a slow oven.

This cake is not easily made, because it requires so much beating and such careful baking. Everything should be prepared before beginning, so that the hand need not be removed from the mixture until it is finished and ready to be put in the pan.

Ribbon Cake.

Sugar,	2 cups.
Butter,	1 cup.
Sweet milk,	1 cup.
Sifted flour,	4 "
Eggs,	4.
Cream of tartar,	1 teaspoonful.
Soda,	½ teaspoonful.

Dissolve soda in a little water, then beat all well together. Bake half of this in two jelly cake pans. To the remaining dough, add

Seeded raisins,	1 cup.
Currants,	2 "
Molasses	2 tablespoonfuls.
Cinnamon,	1 teaspoonful.
Allspice,	1 "
Cloves,	1 "

Bake this in a pan of the same size as jelly cake tins. Lay the three loaves together, the fruit loaf in the middle with a little icing between them.

Chocolate Cake.

Eggs, (3 yolks 1 white),	3.
Sugar,	2 cups.
Milk,	1 "
Sifted flour,	3 "
Butter,	2 tablespoonfuls.
Baking powder,	2 teaspoonfuls.

Sift baking powder with flour, mix all thoroughly and bake in jelly cake tins.

FILLING.

Eggs, (whites only)	2.
Powdered sugar,	1 cup.
Grated chocolate, or Phillips' cocoa,	½ "

Beat all well together and put between layers and on the top.

SNOW CAKE.

Sugar,	1 cup.
Butter,	½ "
Flour,	1½ "
Sweet milk,	½ "
Eggs (whites only),	4.
Baking powder,	2 teaspoonfuls.

Beat all well together. Flavor to taste. Bake in a quick oven.

CREAM CAKE.

Sugar,	2 cups.
Sifted flour,	2 "
Good cream,	1 "
Eggs,	2.
Baking powder,	2 small teaspoonfuls.

Beat all well together. Bake in loaf.

QUICK CAKE.

Sugar,	1 cup.
Butter	2 tablespoonfuls.
Eggs	2
Sweet milk	½ cup
Sifted flour	1½ cups
Baking powder	1 teaspoonful

Beat whites and yolks of eggs separately. Mix all

well together and bake in quick oven. May be eaten warm.

My Grandmother's Sayings.

My grandmother used to say, "There is a great deal of nonsense talked about cake-making. It is not half the worry that people think. If you are in haste or have unexpected company, just do this."

Then she would carefully lay aside the "big Bible," take off her spectacles, put on a large checked apron and go out into a kitchen as large as the whole of a modern flat. She would break the eggs into the bowl, measure into it flour, sugar, etc., stir all around quickly a few times, pour into a pan and set into the oven. This would take about five minutes and the cake was always good.

This will do with simple recipes, but very elaborate ones must be made carefully.

PIE.

REMARKS ABOUT IT.

"What you don't know, don't worry you."
LIZZIE.

AMERICAN PIE.

"Tough and indigestible above; more tough and indigestible below, with untold horrors between'"
THE ENGLISH TOURIST.

PIE.

The greatest obstacle to the advancement of the American nation. It is making a race of dyspeptics.
THE REFORMER.

As this book is not written to retard progress, but to help it on, there are in it no recipes for the ordinary pie, the crust shortened with lard, because other desserts are more wholesome. But English fruit pies, sometimes called by us "Apple Cobblers," "Peach Cobblers," etc., are very good. Below are general directions for making them.

ENGLISH FRUIT PIES.

Take a deep earthen dish and fill it with any fruit, adding sugar, spices or any seasoning desired. Lay over the top of this a thick biscuit crust and bake until well done. Serve with cream or with some liquid sauce. Fruit pies made in this way have no heavy undercrust, soaked with fat and juice, but are very appetizing and digestible.

JELLY.

GENERAL DIRECTIONS.

1. The fruit must not be too ripe.
2. The juice should drip from the bag without pressure.
3. There should be equal parts of juice and sugar, cup for cup.
4. The jelly is cooked enough when it drops clear from the spoon.
5. Great care must be taken to skim well after juice and sugar boil up together.
6. Put into jelly glasses. When cool and settled, lay over the top a piece of writing paper cut to fit smoothly and dipped in good brandy or alcohol. Then screw on the tops.

CURRANT JELLY.

Take a box of good, sound currants and pick them over carefully but do not remove stems. Put them into preserving kettle, warm them all through and mash with a spoon. Have a bag of cheese cloth, fill it with fruit, tie up and let the juice drain from it. The jelly is better if the fruit is not squeezed. When well drained, measure the juice. Boil for ten minutes, then add an equal quantity of sugar, cup for cup and boil ten minutes longer, or until it will drop from the end of a spoon.

Crab Apple Jelly.

Wash and cut into halves nice crab apples. Put over fire in preserving kettle with a little boiling water. Stir constantly to keep from burning. When done, put the jelly into a bag, and let it drip from it. When the juice stops dripping, add to it an equal amount of sugar, measuring first a cup of juice, then of sugar. Boil until done. This takes longer than currant jelly. It is done when it drips clear from the spoon.

Raspberry Jelly.

Pick over thoroughly and wash two boxes (10 quarts) of raspberries. Put in preserving kettle and let them warm up to form juice, then in bag to drain. To every cup of juice add one cup of sugar. Boil hard ten minutes, skimming carefully the while. When done, the jelly will drop from the spoon.

Grape Jelly.

Mash well some sour grapes and put into a preserving kettle with a little water to cook. Stir to keep from burning. When done put into a bag, hang the bag and let the juice drain until clear, then add sugar, cup for cup, and cook until done. This jelly requires more cooking than any other kind.

Lemon Jelly.

Take one half box Cox's gelatine and soak in one half cup cold water. When soaked, add one coffee cup sugar, juice of two lemons and one rind. Allow it to remain in the kettle about two minutes. Then strain through a linen cloth into molds.

Raspberry Jam.

To 12 lbs. nice fruit, add 6 lbs. sugar and let it stand twenty-four hours. Then put into preserving kettle and boil up well. Add 5 lbs. more of sugar and boil three-fourths of an hour, stirring all the time. When well done, put in jelly glasses and seal.

Blackberry Jam.

May be made in the same way.

Pickled Figs.

Figs,	6 lbs.
Sugar,	3 "
Vinegar (good,)	1 qt.

A little cloves, allspice and cinnamon in a bag. Let the figs stand over night in a weak solution of salt and water. Wipe well in the morning. Let the sugar and vinegar become scalding hot, put in the figs and boil until soft. Take out carefully, put into a jar and pour the liquor over. Repeat this process two or three times.

Bottled Peaches.

To thirty lbs. of peaches, pared and halved, take 15 lbs. sugar. To one-half the sugar add enough water to melt it. When it boils, drop in half the peaches, let them remain on the stove five minutes, then bottle. Use other half of the fruit in the same way. (Always have bottles hot.)

Bottled Apricots.

Same recipe as for peaches.

Apricot Marmalade.

To 10 lbs. apricots, pared and stoned, use 7 lbs. sugar.

Add to the apricots one-half the sugar and let them stand over night. Then put on stove, and let them come to boiling point. Then add remainder of the sugar and boil four hours. One-half hour before it is done, add 1 doz. blanched and chopped apricot stones. Put in jelly glasses.

BOTTLED PEARS.

Pare fruit and cut in halves. To every 10 lbs. of fruit use 7 lbs. sugar. Add to sugar one pint boiling water and juice of one lemon. Boil to a syrup. Then add the fruit. Let it cook about one-half hour. Watch carefully.

Some prefer cooking pears about fifteen minutes in clear water before putting in the syrup.

CANNED FRUIT.

Use glass jars and clean them thoroughly. Prepare the fruit, which should not be too ripe, by paring, stoning or whatever is necessary. As the fruit is prepared, place it carefully in the jars, taking care not to break it. Prepare the syrup, sweet according to the acidity of the fruit, and the taste. Boil and skim the syrup. Set the jars in a boiler prepared for canning. If that cannot be procured, take a common boiler. Lay a board in the bottom of it and set the jars filled with the fruit in the boiler, pouring more water around them to about half their height. Put the covers on loosely, but do not screw them down. As soon as the water is hot, pour on hot syrup and cook them twenty minutes. Then fill with syrup to the brim and screw on the tops. Take out of boiler, and set to cool. If not perfectly air-tight, they will leak and the process must be repeated.

DRINKS.

COFFEE.

Buy Mocha or Java coffee ground coarse. Take one tablespoonful for every person and one for the pot. Beat up an egg and mix some or all of it with the coffee. Then stir up the mixture well with two tablespoonfuls of cold water. When well mixed, pour on the boiling water about ten minutes before serving. Keep hot but do not let it boil.

COFFEE, NO. 2.

MADE WITH COLD WATER.

Take coffee in the same proportions as above according to the number of persons. Stir it up thoroughly with a little cold water, just enough to soak the grains. When thoroughly soaked, add a cup of cold water for every person and one for the pot. Mix all thoroughly, place over a hot fire and take off as soon as it boils. It will be clear as amber and very good. This is an excellent way to make coffee over a spirit lamp.

In buying coffee instead of all Java, many persons prefer a mixture of one-third Mocha and two-thirds Java. Those who are fond of strong coffee sometimes prefer one-third Costa Rica and two-thirds Java. Leading grocers now often make their own mixtures, called "Blended Coffee." Always have the coffee berry freshly ground or the aroma escapes and the delicious flavor is lost.

Cocoa Shells.

This is not a favorite drink, but when well made is very good, especially for delicate stomachs. Put two handfuls of shells into a pot and pour over them one pint of boiling water. Boil well for at least one-half hour, then add one pint of good milk. Let it just boil up, after adding the milk. If too strong, add more milk.

Chocolate.

Reliable directions for making chocolate are printed on the packages.

Tea.

Have an earthen tea-pot, heat it well and measure into it one teaspoonful of tea for every person, and one for the pot. Pour boiling water over this, one cup for every spoonful of tea if it is to be of good strength. Let it stand in a warm place. Never boil tea; it makes a bitter and unwholesome drink. Let the water just boil before pouring it over. Tea well made is a fragrant and refreshing drink. Do not buy green teas for they are colored and sometimes poisonous.

BILL OF FARE FOR A WEEK.

SUNDAY.

BREAKFAST.

Fruit,
    Oat Meal Mush with Cream,
        Broiled Chops,
            Graham Gems, Coffee,

DINNER.

Vermicelli Soup,
    Shrimp Salad,
        Split-back Chickens, and Currant Jelly,
        Green Peas, Beets, Potatoes,
            Snow pudding, Angel Food,
                Fresh Fruit,
                    Black Coffee.

SUPPER.

Cold Chicken,
    Bread and Butter, Cake,
        Fruit, Tea or Chocolate.

MONDAY.

BREAKFAST.

Baked Apples,
> Farina Mush with Cream,
>> Hash and Omelet,
>>> Muffins, Coffee.

DINNER.

Tomato Soup,
> Lettuce Salad,
>> Broiled Porter-house Steak,
>>> Sweet Potatoes, String Beans,
>>>> Lemon Meringue,
>>>>> Fresh Fruit,
>>>>>> Black Coffee.

SUPPER.

Stewed Peaches,
> Bread and Butter, Cake,
>> Tea, Chocolate.

TUESDAY.

Breakfast.

Breakfast Delight, with Cream,

Brains a la Creme,

Saratoga Potatoes,

Corn Bread,

Coffee.

Dinner.

Bean Soup,

Salad, Crab on Lettuce,

Boiled Leg of Mutton, Caper Sauce,

Pilaf, Turnips, Potatoes,

Queen of Puddings,

Sliced Peaches,

Black Coffee.

Supper.

Bread and Butter,

Canned Pears, Jelly, Cake,

Cocoa Shells, Tea.

WEDNESDAY.

Breakfast.

Graham Mush with Cream,
    Stewed Prunes,
        Poached Eggs on Toast,
            Cream Potatoes,
                Pop Overs, Coffee.

Dinner.

Oyster Soup.
    Lettuce and Tomato Salad,
        Roast Veal with Cream Gravy,
           Mashed Potatoes, Cauliflower,
              Apple Whip, Fruit,
                  Black Coffee.

Supper.

Buttered Toast,
    Canned Apricots,
        Cake, Tea or Cocoa (Phillips).

THURSDAY.

BREAKFAST.

Rolled Oats with Cream.

Baked Pears.

Cod-fish Cakes, Eggs, (Jellied.)

Brown Bread, Coffee.

DINNER.

Bouillon.

Chicken Salad.

Roast Beef.

Baked Potatoes, Asparagus.

English Plum Pudding,

Nuts and Raisins.

Black Coffee.

SUPPER.

Parker House Rolls.

Baked Apple Sauce, Cake.

Chocolate or Tea.

FRIDAY.

BREAKFAST.

Melon.

    Cracked Wheat with Cream.

        Picked-up Codfish, Sweet Breads.

            Gems, Coffee.

DINNER.

Rice Tomato Soup.

    Salad, Cold Slaw.

        Fish, Roast Beef, (from Thursday.)

            Potatoes, Spinach, Beets.

            Ice cream, Water Melon Cake.

                Fruit, Black Coffee.

SUPPER.

Brown and White Bread.

    Jelly Cake.

        Raspberry Jam.

            Tea or Coffee.

SATURDAY.

BREAKFAST.

Fruit.
Oat Meal and Breakfast Delight with Cream.
Ham and Eggs.
Baking Powder Biscuits.
Coffee

DINNER.

Mutton Broth.
Salad.
Quail on Toast.
Sweet Potatoes, Corn.
Jelly.
English Fruit Pie with Cream.

SUPPER.

Buns, Bread.
Apricot Marmalade.
Cake.
Chocolate.

For those who prefer dinner at night, the dishes given for supper may be used for noon luncheon, with the addition of cold meats and entrees, soups, chops, etc. The supper menus are designedly made very simple, as those who prefer a midday dinner generally wish light suppers.

FOOD FOR INVALIDS.

RAW BEEF SOUP.

Chop fine one pound of raw beef, put it in a bottle with one pint of water and five drops of muriatic acid. Let this stand in a cool place all night. In the morning set the bottle in a pan of water at 110 degrees F., for about two hours. Strain through a cloth until the mass is nearly dry. If the raw taste be objectionable, the beef to be used should be roasted quickly on one side, then make as above. This soup may be substituted for milk when the latter is called for, but cannot be taken.

BEEF TEA.—(Best way.)

Three pounds of beef cut into dice and thrown into three pints of cold water. Let it stand three hours. Add one-half teaspoonful salt, then cover and put it on a slow fire. Let it simmer, but never boil, until the quantity is reduced one-half. This will take six hours at least. Strain and set aside until next day, when skim, season, and serve hot. It should be perfectly clear and of a golden brown color.

BEEF TEA, NO. 2.

A QUICK WAY TO MAKE BEEF TEA.

Cut one-half pound of beef into dice, and put it into a wide mouthed bottle with just cold water enough to cover it. Cork the bottle, and put it in a sauce pan of cold water over a slow fire. When the water in the sauce pan boils, the tea is made. Strain, skim, season and serve hot. This makes about half a cup full.

Beef Tea, No. 3.

Half pound of beef chopped fine, and soaked in half pint cold water with a little salt, for ten minutes. Then heat it slowly to boiling point, and let it boil three minutes. Strain, skim, season, and serve hot.

Beef Tea, No. 4.

BEEF TEA THAT THE MOST DELICATE STOMACH CAN RETAIN.

One pound of beef cut into dice and thrown into one pint cold water, with a pinch of salt. Add four drops of hydro chloric acid, cover, and let it stand half an hour. Skim, strain, season, and serve hot. Only to be given with the Doctor's consent.

Beef Juice.

Take one pound of beef cut into dice, and throw it into half a pint cold water. Let it stand twelve hours. Then strain, skim, heat quickly with a little salt, and serve hot. with a half slice thin, hot toast.

Beef Juice, No. 2.

Boil for one minute, one pound of beef. Then grate it fine by rubbing and tearing it on a large grater. Rub this through a sieve and you have a thickish liquid which can be drank, and yet contains the whole nourishment of the beef. Heat quickly with a little salt and serve.

Beef Tea and Egg.

Beat a raw egg a little and stir it into a half pint of hot beef tea.

Egg Nogg.

Beat up well the yolk of an egg. Add slowly one tablespoonful of boiling water. Beat again. Add one teaspoonful of sugar. Beat again. Add slowly one tablespoonful of brandy, beating constantly. Have ready the white of the egg, beaten lightly. Stir it in thoroughly, and serve at once.

Egg Nogg, No. 2.

One egg; One tumbler of milk;
One dessertspoonful of brandy;
 "   "   " sugar.

Carefully scald the milk and let it afterwards become cold. Beat the sugar and eggs together to a froth, put into a glass, add the brandy and fill up with the milk. Can be made quickly if desired without boiling the milk.

Baked Milk.

Put the milk into a stone-ware jar and cover with foolscap writing paper tied over it. Set it in a moderate oven for two or three hours according to quantity. This is very delicate when made properly. Experience will guide as to heat of oven. The paper allows for slow evaporation.

Macaroni and Milk.

Take three pieces of curled macaroni, soak in pint of

warmed milk until quite swollen and soft. Add pinch of salt, and boil slowly for twenty minutes.

Milk Punch.

One tumblerful of milk; two dessertspoonfuls brandy. Sweeten the milk well and stir in the brandy thoroughly. Keep very cold with ice.

Kumys.

Three quarts fresh, rich milk; Three quarts hot water; Half a pound of white sugar; one tablespoonful of good yeast. Dissolve the sugar in the hot water, add this to the milk, and let them cool until lukewarm. Now, slowly and carefully stir in the yeast. Set the crock containing this in a warm place to rise as you would bread. In five or six hours, it will be slightly sparkling, and small bubbles will rise to the surface when stirred. When it reaches this stage, put it into *stout* bottles, tie down the corks, and set bottles in a cool place, in the refrigerator or on the floor of a cool cellar. A thick mass (the caseine) will form on the surface; once or twice a day, for several days, the bottle should be well shaken, and this will fall in a powder to the bottom. When two days old, it is ready for use, although it will keep for a much longer time, and may be used when a week or more old. It is best, however, when two to four days old. Care must be used in opening. Use a champagne faucet if possible.

Corn Meal Gruel.

Take a quart of boiling water, stir into it 2 tablespoonfuls of corn-meal and ½ teaspoonful of salt. Boil hard for 1 hour, stirring constantly. Milk may be added to s, if agreeable to the invalid.

FARINA GRUEL.

Take a pint of boiling water and stir into it 2 tablespoonfuls of farina and ½ teaspoonful of salt. Stir constantly while it boils half an hour.

OAT MEAL GRUEL.

Take a pint of Irish oat-meal and pour upon it a quart of cold water. Let it stand three hours, stirring occasionally. When well soaked drain off the water and put the water into a double kettle to boil, adding 1½ teaspoonful of salt. Let it boil slowly for one hour. Milk may be added, if agreeable to the patient.

MILK GRUEL.—(With flour.)

Put a pint of milk in a double kettle and let it boil. Blend a tablespoonful of flour and ⅓ teaspoonful of salt with a little water, and stir it into the boiling milk, stirring constantly until it thickens.

HUSBANDS.

A RECIPE FOR COOKING HUSBANDS.

One of the lectures before the Baltimore Cooking School recently gave this recipe for cooking husbands: "A good many husbands are utterly spoiled by mismanagement. Some women keep them constantly in hot water. Others let them freeze by their carelessness and indifference. Some keep them in a stew by irritating ways and words; others roast them. Some keep them in a pickle all their lives. It cannot be supposed that any husband will be tender and good, managed in this way, but he is truly delicious when properly treated. In selecting your husband you should not be guided by the silvery appearance, as in buying a mackerel, nor by the golden tint, as if you wanted a salmon. Be sure to select him yourself, as tastes differ. Do not go to market for him, as the best are always brought to your door. It is far better to have none, unless you will patiently learn how to cook him. A preserving kettle of the finest porcelain is the best, but if you have nothing but an earthen pipkin it will do, with care. See that the linen in which you wrap him is nicely washed and mended, with the required number of buttons and strings tightly sewed on. Tie him in the kettle by a strong silk cord called comfort, as the one called duty is apt to be weak. Make a clear, steady fire out of love, neatness and cheerfulness. Set him as near this as seems to agree with him. If he sputters and fizzes, do not be anxious; some husbands do this till they are quite done. Add a little sugar, in the form of what confectioners call kisses, but no vinegar or pepper on any account. A little spice improves him, but it must be used with judgment. Do not stick any sharp instrument into him to see if he is becoming tender. Stir him gently, watching the while, lest he lie too flat and close to the kettle, and so become useless. You can not fail to know when he is done. If thus treated, you will find him very reliable, agreeing nicely with you and the children, and he will keep as long as you want, unless you become careless and set him in too cold a place."

GENERAL INDEX.

	PAGE
How to select good Flour	9
BREAD	10
White Bread	10
Graham Bread	11
Boston Brown Bread	11
Graham Gems	12
Muffins	12
Breakfast Rolls	13
Parker House Rolls	13
Baking Powder Biscuits	14
White Gems	14
Hygienic Batter Cakes	14
Rice Griddle Cakes	15
Welch Griddle Cakes	15
Sally Lunn	16
Pop Overs	16
Waffles	16
Corn Bread	17
MUSH	18
Corn Meal Mush	18
Fried Mush	18
Graham Mush	18
Sago Mush	18
Germea Mush	19
Farina Mush	19
Whole Wheat Mush	19
Breakfast Delight	19
Rolled Oats	19
Boiled Rice	20
Cracked Wheat Mush	20
Hominy	20
BEEF	21
How to tell good Beef	21
Roast Beef	21

	PAGE
How to buy Beefsteak	22
How to Broil a Beefsteak	22
Beef a La Mode	23
Baked Beefsteak	23
How to select corned Beef	24
Corned Beef	24
Spanish tomato beefste'k	24
Beef Heart	24
Yorkshire Pudding	24
Irish Stew	25
MUTTON	25
How to Choose Good Mutton	25
Roast leg of Mutton or Lamb	25
Mutton Chops	26
Roast Mutton or Lamb	26
Minced Mutton or Lamb	26
Scalloped Mutton	26
VEAL	26
How to choose good Veal	26
Roast Weal	27
Veal Cutlets	27
Veal Stew	27
Veal Loaf	27
Veal Fricassee	28
Meat Souffle	28
Stuffed Veal	28
Sweet Breads	28
Calf's or Sheep's Brains	29
Scrambled Brains	29
PORK	29
How to Select Pork	29
Pork Chops	29

LIZZIE'S COOK BOOK.

	PAGE
Ham	30
Devilled Ham	30
Spare Ribs	30
Roast Pork	30
Liver	30
Kidney Stew	31
Ham and Eggs	31

SOUP STOCK 31

Bouillon	32
Ox Tail Soup	32
Tomato Soup	32
Beef Tea or Broth for Invalids	32
Bean Soup	33
Potato Soup	33
Tomato Cream Soup	33
Corn Soup for 12 Persons	33
Mutton Broth	34
Clam Chowder	34
Clam Soup	34
Oyster Soup	34
Lentil Soup	35
Mock Turtle Soup	35
Chicken Broth	36
Turkey Soup	36
Salsify or Oyster Plant Soup	36

FOWLS 37

How to choose a good Turkey	37
Roast Turkey	37
To make the gravy	38
Boned Turkey	38
How to select Good Chickens	38
Roast Chicken	39
Split-back Chicken	39
Fried Chicken	39
Chicken Fricassee	39
Chicken Pie	40
Quail	41
Fried Quail	41
Broiled Quail	41
Signs by which you may know Young Ducks	41
Roast Duck	42
Tame Pigeon	42
English Snipe	42

	PAGE
FISH	43
How to Choose Good Salmon	43
Boiled Salmon	43
Fried Salmon	43
Baked Shad	43
Shad Fried	44
Silver Smelt	44
Broiled Smelt	44
Fresh Mackerel	44
Salt Mackerel	44
Lake Trout Broiled	44
Lake Trout Fried	45
Cod Fish	45
Salt Cod Fish	45

SALADS 46

Chicken Salad	46
Salad Dressing	46
Potato Salad	47
Tomato and Lettuce Salad	47
Shrimp Salad	47
Crab Salad	47

SANDWICHES .. 48

Ham	48
Cottage Cheese	48
Boned Turkey	48
Egg	48

VEGETABLES.... 49

Boiled Potatoes	49
Scalloped Potatoes	49
Lyonnaise Potatoes	50
Cream Potatoes	50
Breakfast Potatoes	50
Boiled Sweet Potatoes	50
Baked Sweet Potatoes	51
Rice as a Vegetable	51
Squash	51
Stuffed Squash	51
Turnips	52
Beets	52
Baked Tomatoes	52
Scalloped Tomatoes	53
Steamed Tomatoes	53
String Beans	53
Lima Beans	54
Green Peas	54

INDEX.

	PAGE		PAGE
Corn Oysters	54	Ice Cream	70
Green Corn	54	Fruit Cream	70
Asparagus	54	Strawberry Cream	70
Spinach	55	Lemon Ice	71
Egg Plant	55	Junket	71
Cauliflower	56	Chocolate Ice Cream	71
Stewed Celery	56	Frozen Peaches	72
Mushrooms	56	Tapioca Ice	72
Succotash	57	Eggs	73
		How to tell Fresh Eggs	73
ENTREES	58	Jellied Eggs	73
Devilled Crab	58	Baked Eggs	73
Fish Croquettes	58	Scrambled Eggs	73
Chicken Croquettes	58	Poached Eggs	74
Scalloped Oysters	59	Fried Eggs	74
Fried Oysters	59	Omelet	74
Broiled Oysters	59	Ham Omelet	75
Stuffed Potatoes	59	Oyster Omelet	75
Corn Fritters	60	Omelet with Jelly	75
Pilaf	60		
		CAKE	76
PICKLES	61		
Chow Chow	61	Angel Food	76
Pickled Peaches	61	Delicate Cake	76
Sweet Pickles	62	Cocoanut Cake	77
Tomato Sauce	62	Hickory-nut Cake	77
Tomato Catsup	62	Silver Cake	78
Chili Sauce	62	Gold Cake	78
		1-2-3-4 Cake	78
PUDDINGS	63	Orange Cake	78
		Jelly Cake	79
Snow Pudding	63	Marble Cake	79
Custard for Snow Pudding	63	Molasses Cake	80
Poor Man's Pudding	64	Cream Puffs	80
Queen of Puddings	64	Fig Cake	81
Apple Whip	64	Wedding Cake	81
Lemon Meringue	65	Genuine Fruit Cake	82
Floating Island	65	Cookies	82
Fruit Tapiocca	65	Molasses Cookies	83
Bavarian Cream	65	Black Cake	83
Steamed Rice	66	Watermelon Cake	84
Coffee Jelly	66	White Sponge Cake	85
Rhubarb Pudding	66	Plain Sponge Cake	85
Baked Custard	67	Pound Cake	85
Souffle Pudding	67	Ribbon Cake	86
Cottage Pudding	68	Chocolate Cake	86
Good Fruit Pudding	68	Snow Cake	87
Strawberry Short Cake	69	Cream Cake	87
Sweet Short Cake	69	Quick Cake	87
Suet Pudding	69	My Grandmother's Sayings	88

	PAGE
PIE	89
American Pie	89
Fruit Pies	89
JELLY	90
Currant Jelley	90
Crab Apple Jelly	91
Raspberry Jelly	91
Grape Jelly	91
Lemon Jelly	91
Raspberry Jam	92
Blackberry Jam	92
Pickled Figs	92
Bottled Peaches	92
Bottled Apricots	92
Apricot Marmalade	92
Bottled Pears	93
CANNED FRUIT	94
DRINKS	95
Coffee	95

	PAGE
Cocoa Shells	96
Chocolate	96
Tea	96
BILL OF FARE FOR A WEEK	97—103
FOOD FOR INVALIDS	104
Raw Beef Soup	104
Beef Tea (Best way)	104
Beet Juice	105
Egg Nogg	106
Beef Tea and Egg	106
Baked Milk	106
Maccaroni and Milk	106
Milk Punch	107
Kumys	107
Corn Meal Gruel	107
Farina Gruel	108
Oatmeal Gruel	108
Milk Gruel (flour)	108
HUSBANDS (How to Cook)	109

ALPHABETICAL INDEX.

	PAGE
Bread	10— 17
Bill of Fare	97—103
Cakes	76— 88
Canned Fruit	94
Drinks	95— 96
Entrees	58— 60
Eggs	73— 75
Fowls	37— 40
Fish	43— 45
Food for Invalids	104—108
Game	41— 42

	PAGE
How to Select Good Flour	9
Husbands	109
Jelly	90— 93
Mush	18— 20
Preface	5— 6
Pickles	61— 62
Puddings	63— 72
Pie	89
Salads	46— 47
Sandwiches	48
Vegetables	49— 57

INDEX TO ADVERTISERS.

	PAGE
W. E. Crossman & Co.	1
Martin & Estraboou	2
Raley & Co.	3
Mrs. Worcester	3
San Jose Mercury	4
Notion Store	60
Women Physicians	61
Rudolph	115
City of San Jose	115

	PAGE
San Jose Herald	116
J. G. Munson	117
Hill & Watkins	117
Charles A. Bothwell	118
W. S. Trader & Co.	118
E. H. Wemple	119
San Jose Tea Co.	119
Mangrum & Otter	120
Gray & Cadwell	120

www.ingramcontent.com/pod-product-compliance
Lightning Source LLC
Chambersburg PA
CBHW021919180426
43199CB00032B/733